HIGH-LEVEL EVERYDA
with Audio CD

by Steven Collins

HIGH-LEVEL STUDENTS OF ENGLISH

You will never find a better series of books to help you improve your vocabulary

ISBN 0-9528358-5-1
978-0-9528358-5-1

www.everydayenglishbooks.com

Montserrat Publishing

MONTSERRAT PUBLISHING

High-Level Everyday English

Copyright © 2013 Steven Collins

First edition 2013
Second edition 2014

Montserrat Publishing

Illustrations
Alex Stead
www.alexsteadart.com
info@alexsteadart.com

Typesetting & Cover Design
Naroa Lizar Redrado
naroa.lizar@gmail.com

Editing and proofreading
Gavin Best
bestgav@hotmail.com

CD recording
Soundmagic Studios
info@soundmagic.co.uk

CD voices
Gavin Best
Steve Collins
Jullian Irvine
Alison Jones
Amanda May

www.everydayenglishbooks.com

To my parents, Bobbie and Gerry Collins

Steven Collins was born in London in 1960. He grew up in Harrow and qualified as a lawyer (solicitor) in 1987, having done a Master's in Law at Trinity Hall, Cambridge. He then decided to make a complete change of career and went into T.E.F.L. (Teaching English as a Foreign Language). Having lived and taught in Italy and Spain, he returned to London in 1993 to write this book and to open his own school in Central London, specialising in practical English for advanced students. However, in 2008 he retired from teaching to concentrate full time on writing and publishing.

Other books by the same author:

Everyday English Series with Audio CD

By Steven Collins

Vocabulary and grammar books for upper-intermediate and advanced students.

Available at all good bookshops and online stores including Amazon.

Book 1

Book 2

Grammar Book (no CD)

www.everydayenglishbooks.com

Introduction
HIGH-LEVEL EVERYDAY ENGLISH
Steven Collins

High-level Everyday English *is the third book in the Practical Everyday English series.*

All the books are designed for students who already have good English, but this third one is especially for those who have reached a very advanced stage in their English studies…but still need a little help with difficult vocabulary.

The method used is the same as in the previous two books, i.e. nearly all examples contain words and expressions which you will have studied either earlier in this book or in the other books. You should aim to study one lesson a week and revise each chapter when you finish it.

I hope, just as in the other books, you will also enjoy listening to the audio CD of the dialogues which appear at the end of each chapter. It will help you a lot in your listening comprehension.

Don't forget to do all the exercises after the dialogues to test yourself on what you have studied in each chapter. They will certainly keep your brain active.

Most importantly, I want you to feel confident and proud of your English. You have come so far already…and this book will help you go a little further.

Wishing you the very best of luck.

Steven Collins

For more information about the Practical Everyday English series, visit:
www.everydayenglishbooks.com

Chapter One
Lesson One

Heyday (A time in the past when someone/something was at his/its best--*generally used to state that this is no longer the case*)

Examples:
*   *In his **heyday** he was the best ad-libber on the stage, but now he is prone to making mistakes and needs to prepare a script beforehand.*
*   *Progressive Rock had its **heyday** in the 1970s. My memory of those days is somewhat blurred because it was a long time ago… and I was paralytic most of the time.*

To keep tight-lipped about something (Not to talk about something; to keep something to oneself, to be secretive)

Examples:
*   *She's **keeping very tight-lipped about** her boyfriend. From what I can gather, he hasn't endeared himself to her friends and family..*
*   *I think he's quite hopeful that business will pick up, but he's **keeping tight-lipped about** it. He doesn't want to come over as complacent.*

To deter (To discourage someone from doing something; to put someone off--*see Practical Everyday English, page 55, meaning iii*)

Examples:
*   *I don't want to **deter** her from what is quite clearly a childhood dream, but she could find herself out of her depth at Cambridge.*
*   *Don't be **deterred** by what your dad says about your plans. He's not so well up on what's going on in the world today, anyway.*

Knee-jerk (Automatic and fast--*used to describe a reaction/response which is generally too fast and therefore negative*)

Examples:
*   *The police now admit that the mistakes they had made were as a result of a **knee-jerk** reaction to relentless media pressure to solve the case…but they resent being accused of incompetence.*

- *It all sounds perfectly plausible to me at this early stage, but I don't want to come out with some **knee-jerk** response that I will live to regret later on.*

Backlash (The negative consequences following an action or event, a hostile reaction)

Examples:
- *There's bound to be a **backlash** against the Government's decision to support the Libyan rebels, despite their current plight.*
- Football News:
  *So far, there has been no **backlash** following on from the manager's sacking. The chairman of the supporters' club agreed that the board couldn't stave off this inevitable action any longer*

*"Progressive Rock had its **heyday** in the 1970s. My memory of those days is somewhat blurred because it was a long time ago… and I was paralytic most of the time." (see page 1)*

Gruelling (Very difficult and tiring, tough)

Examples:
- My son said that the exams are going to be very **gruelling**. However, I'm quite hopeful he'll get through them.
- I went in for the London Marathon this year and I have to say I've never been through such a **gruelling** experience in my life; mind you, I was consoled by the fact that I did it in less than four hours.

Mug (A fool/idiot, a gullible person--see *Practical Everyday English, page 104. Also note the expression "**a mug's game**", which means a foolish activity*)

Examples:
- I now realise that in trying to endear myself to my staff I've actually alienated most of them. I've been a real **mug**.
- You're a **mug** if you believe his version of events was not embellished.
- In his heyday, he was the top lawyer in the country, but now he has deemed the legal profession to be a **mug's game**.

To mug someone, mugging (To rob someone; robbery of a person-- *note the expression "**to mug up on something**" which means to study, revise, do research on something for a specific purpose*)

Examples:
- When she was **mugged** on her way home last week, her gut reaction was to scream. It's just as well she did because it scared the mugger off.
- This area of London is prone to **mugging**; I would steer clear of it if I were you.
- I can't afford to make a fool of myself ad-libbing a speech. I'll have to **mug up on** the subject beforehand.

Gulf (A big gap/difference of opinion)

Examples:
- The **gulf** between the two main political parties on the issue of the rise in muggings in the capital has widened considerably in recent months. But nothing will deter the Prime Minister from sticking to his policy of zero tolerance towards violent criminals.
- There is a **gulf** of class and quality between the two Manchester clubs and the other teams in the Premier league. Any mug can see that.

To spark (To provoke/stimulate--*used for a reaction rather than a person. You cannot "spark" someone*)

Examples:
- The Managing Director's comments about many of the staff not being up to scratch are bound to **spark** a backlash amongst the company's employees.
- The Health Minister's report has **sparked** an outburst of frustration and anger within the nursing profession.

To lose it (To lose one's temper, to get furiously angry and lose control) **Colloquial**

Examples:
- I completely **lost it**. It was an angry, knee-jerk reaction which I was unable to control. I regret it now, but don't want to dwell on it.
- We had embarked on a gruelling military campaign during which the captain **lost it** with me and the other soldiers on several occasions.

Lesson Two

Blunder (A big mistake)

Examples:
- Newspaper headline:
  *Doctor's confession to major **blunders** sparks outrage amongst patients.*
- *The Minister for Employment accepts that he made a huge **blunder** when he said that women need to be deterred from taking so much sick-leave. It's quite unusual for a politician to make such an admission; they usually keep tight-lipped about such things.*

To take the bull by the horns (To deal with/take control of a situation/problem properly)

Examples:
- *Stop dithering! If you want to narrow the gulf in ability between these two directors, you need to **take the bull by the horns** and act now.*
- *If we had **taken the bull by the horns** at the beginning, there wouldn't have been such a backlash from the members of the committee.*

To overlook (To ignore/forget about an error or fault; to fail to notice)

Examples:
- Boss to employee:
  *I will **overlook** your persistent lateness if you promise to keep tight-lipped about my accounts.*
- *I do not understand how these blunders in the contract could have been **overlooked** by both sets of lawyers. Extraordinary!*

To be wary of (To distrust, to be suspicious of)

Examples:
- *I'd be very **wary** of him; he tends to lose it when he doesn't get his own way.*
- *The doctor advised my mother to be slightly **wary of** this medication. It has been known to cause blurred vision.*

- She was **wary of** going into such a strange business with no relevant experience. It all seemed a bit of a mug's game.

To plug (To promote the sale of something by talking about it in public--*especially a book, record or film. Note also the following two expressions:* **"to plug the gap"**, *which means to fill in any gaps of knowledge or information, and* **"to plug away"**, *which means to continue working hard at something. See the last two examples below.*)

Examples:
- I will put in a good word for you with some literary journalists I know, in the hope that they **plug** your next book in their weekly newspaper columns.
- Most pop musicians these days are always trying to **plug** their latest releases. It's a trait that I don't find particularly endearing.
- This exam revision course will **plug any gaps** in your knowledge of chemistry. You'll still have to mug up on the basics, though.
- During his divorce, when things were looking bleak, he kept **plugging away** at his songwriting. It helped him come through this dark period of his life.

"I'd be very **wary** of him; he tends to lose it when he doesn't get his own way." *(see page 5)*

To have the gift of the gab (To be a good talker; to be good at convincing people to buy or do things)

Examples:
- You have to have the **gift of the gab** if you want to be good at ad-libbing on the stage.
- It's clear that she has the **gift of the gab**, which is why no-one needed to show her the ropes when she began her job in telephone sales.

To step something up (To increase the speed, amount or intensity of something--*note also the expression "to step up to the plate/challenge" which means to assume responsibility for something*)

Examples:
- The Prime Minister resents the fact that the leader of the Opposition is **stepping up** pressure on him to put in a good word for the British manufacturing industry at the next European Union meeting of heads of government. He feels he hardly needs reminding to give the country a plug.
- On paper it seems that an easy solution to dealing with rising crime in this city is to take the bull by the horns and **step up** police numbers. But this might be seen by some as an expensive knee-jerk reaction at a time of public sector cutbacks.
- It's clear that Julie has the gift of the gab when it comes to dealing with customers, but I'm not sure she is ready, willing and able to **step up to the plate/challenge** and take on a managerial role.

To step down (To resign from office or an important position)

Examples:
- Having made so many blunders in recent times, he had no option but to **step down**. However, he said it wouldn't deter him from looking for similar work in the future.
- I reckon he's had his heyday and it's time for him to **step down**. Politics is a mug's game anyway.

Farce, farcical (A ridiculous, absurd situation; laughable; very badly organised--
*note that a "farce" is also a light comedy performed at the theatre. It is usually fast moving, has
an improbable plot and often concerns mistaken identity or a complete misunderstanding of a
situation*)

Examples:

- *The referee turned the game into a **farce** when he sent off two
  players for swearing but somehow overlooked three dangerous tackles.*
- *The funeral arrangements were **farcical**. They got the deceased's
  body mixed up with someone else's and turned up at the wrong
  cemetery. The poor widow was beyond consolation, and her daughter
  completely lost it with the funeral director.*

In the wake of (Following on from an event or action)

Examples:

- ***In the wake of** the Home Secretary's blunders last week, the
  Prime Minister has had to take the bull by the horns. He could do
  without these problems, especially in light of last month's fiasco
  concerning the Deputy Prime Minister.*
- *There are many things which we cannot afford to overlook **in the
  wake of** the farce which went on in the boardroom last Friday.*

8

Lesson Three

To mope (To feel a little depressed and apathetic--*when used with "around/about", it means to walk around with no purpose because of unhappiness or boredom*)

Examples:
- *I nearly lost it with him today. He has sat in his room all day **moping**, and he didn't lift a finger to help me all weekend.*
- *I know you've had a gruelling week, but it's no good **moping** <u>around</u> wallowing in self-pity. Keep plugging away and you'll see the rewards will come.*

To turn something around (To change something for the better; to improve one's life)

Examples:
- *John has really **turned** this football club **around.** The way the old manager ran things was a farce. We're all so glad he was asked to step down.*
- *I thought my life was doomed before I met Michael. I was a bit wary of him at first, but it is truly amazing how he has **turned** my life **around**.*

To do oneself down (To have a low opinion of oneself; to believe one is not capable of doing something)

Examples:
- *Don't **do yourself down** all the time. You shouldn't be so easily deterred from having high aspirations.*
- *I don't know what sparked this current episode of self-doubt. She must stop moping around and **doing herself down.** She's got so much going for her.*

To crave, have/get a craving for something (To need something desperately--*usually something pleasant*--to have a strong desire/fancy for something--*note that pregnant women are well known for having "cravings" for strange combinations of food at irregular hours*)

Examples:
- *She takes after her mother, in that she **craves** affection. I'm not very hopeful she'll find it in her new boyfriend.*

- When I was pregnant with Jake, I would often **have/get a craving for** sausages and ice cream. My husband Sam never seemed to notice, as he was plugging away at his work on his laptop.

To give someone a dressing-down (To scold, to tell off--*note that this expression is generally more formal and serious than "to tell off"*)

Examples:
- If he doesn't manage to turn this company around by the end of the year, the shareholders are going to **give him** a very sharp **dressing-down**.
- In the wake of such a heavy defeat against their bitterest rivals, the boss **gave** the whole team a **dressing-down**.

To lose one's marbles (To lose one's mind/mental faculties--*generally used in a humorous way and not to describe serious dementia. Note also the expression "**to lose the plot**", which means to lose the ability to understand what is going on, or to go a little bit crazy and over-the-top*)

Examples:
- It was a farcical situation: neither of us could remember the other's name. At 49 years old, we are both clearly beginning to **lose our marbles**.
- A: Recently I've been prone to getting up early on Sunday morning thinking it was Monday. I must be **losing my marbles**.

  B: And time for you to step down as boss of the company?
- If the Leader of the Opposition thinks that he could turn the economy round with his farcical policies, he really has **lost the plot.**

To opt (To make a choice--*followed by "for" when preceding a noun. Also note the expression "**to opt out of**", which means to make a decision not to participate in a particular system*)

Examples:
- They **opted** to send their son to the local private school because of the wide gulf that exists between the state and independent sectors.
- We were overwhelmed with choices, none of which was overlooked. However, in the end we **opted** <u>for</u> the project that would give us fewer teething problems.
- In the wake of Government cutbacks to the National Health Service, some small hospitals have decided to **opt out of** local health authority schemes.

To be at the cutting edge of something (To be at the forefront of modern development)

Examples:
- We are always doing ourselves down in this country despite the fact that others view us as **being at the cutting edge** of many specialist hi-tech industries.
- Our aim in launching this new TV station was not to spark controversy, but **to be at the cutting edge of** today's media.
  (see picture below)

To banish (To throw someone out; to send someone away; to remove a thought from one's mind)

Examples:
- He should be **banished** from this country so that he can no longer plug his Nazi propaganda on our shores. I'm very wary of people like him.
- A: Do you think I might be sacked over this last blunder I made?
- B: **Banish** the thought!

A NEWSPAPER ARTICLE ABOUT PUBLIC TRANSPORT IN LONDON

Some people say that public transport, as we know it, has had its heyday, and that instead of sitting around moping and whingeing, politicians, many of whom ought to have stepped down years ago, should take the bull by the horns and, as far as transport is concerned, opt out of public ownership altogether.

Let's face it: the system as it exists today is a complete farce and is doomed to even more delays and overcrowding. But is the Government right to keep plugging the private investment option, which appears to be a knee-jerk reaction to the public transport problems we had last Christmas? In the wake of recent financial and administrative disasters, privatisation of the national railways has sparked a public backlash against multinational companies investing in transport.

London should be at the cutting edge of modern Europe and it is crucial that the widening gulf that exists between this city and other European capitals should be addressed. In particular, the Government needs to look into the possibility of launching a new funding policy for London Underground without overlooking the blunders that have been made in other areas of national transport. They should not be deterred by the failure of previous governments.

CONVERSATION BETWEEN TWO LAWYERS

PETER: *I don't know about you but I've had a gruelling day…and I nearly lost it with a few annoying clients.*

COLIN: *Yes, I know how you feel. I almost gave one of the youngsters in the office a dressing-down but thought better of it. Being a solicitor is a mug's game. Why do we do it?*

PETER: *The money! Look, my best friend's an English teacher and he's totally skint. Yes, I crave more time with my family, and if I had the gift of the gab, I'd be in real estate, but deep down I'd be quite wary of changing my profession so late in life…when I'm beginning to lose my marbles.*

COLIN: *Well, I suppose I'm always doing the legal profession down and I sometimes forget that being made a partner has turned my life around from a financial point of view…and I still get a buzz out of mugging up on certain specialist areas of the law.*

PETER: *And let's be honest: all this stuff people come out with about money not being important and that capitalism should be banished to the history books is utter nonsense. They keep very tight-lipped when their own promotion comes up for discussion.*

COLIN: *All very true…but nevertheless, I can't wait to call it a day and retire to Spain.*

Chapter One: Exercise

CHOOSE THE CORRECT WORD FROM THOSE IN GREEN
Answers on page 139

1. Apparently, the Managing Director of Railtrack was given a ᵃ(backlash/dressing- down/ blunder/gulf) by the Minister of Transport, and was ordered to ᵇ(mug up/spark/crave/step up) safety procedures on the railways.

2. I think this actor has definitely had his ᵃ(heyday/dressing-down/gulf/blunders). In a recent television interview he seemed to be ᵇ(tight-lipped/moping/losing his marbles/doing down).

3. A: If you want to get on in the world of marketing, it's crucial that you have the ᵃ(gulf/ blunders/backlash/gift of the gab).
   B: Very true, but you also need the patience and courtesy not to ᵇ(lose it/dress down/step down/keep tight-lipped) with people who are making your life difficult.

4. It made me cringe with embarrassment listening to him ᵃ(deter/mope/crave/plug) his latest book on Radio 4. Doesn't he realise that he's completely out of touch with the general public? It was obvious to anyone listening that he has ᵇ(mugged up/taken the bull by the horns/lost the plot/turned his life around).

5. One cannot ᵃ(crave/overlook/be wary of/plug) the fact that there have been major ᵇ(blunders/ knee-jerk reactions/farces/sparks) at senior management level.

6. The negotiations for creating a faster, safer tube service for London have turned into a complete ᵃ(blunder/backlash/farce/gulf). There is now a massive ᵇ(craving/opting out/knee-jerk response/gulf) between the politicians on one side and the unions on the other.

7. ᵃI don't know why you keep ᵃ(opting out/sparking debate/craving/doing yourself down). It's amazing how you've managed to ᵇ(deter yourself/turn your life around/give yourself a dressing-down/keep tight-lipped) in such a short space of time.

8. ᵃ(In the wake of/Opting out of/Losing one's marbles/Banishing) the Government's decision to raise taxes, there has been a ᵇ(heyday/stepping up/backlash/farce) amongst business leaders.

9. Instead of ᵃ(gruelling/moping/craving/overlooking) around on your own all day wallowing in misery, why don't you ᵇ(take the bull by the horns/dress it down/keep tight-lipped/have the gift of the gab) and get out of the house to enjoy the nice weather? Life is for living.

10. I think she might have been asked to ᵃ(step up/step down/do down/overlook) by the Board of Directors, but she is keeping very ᵇ(wary/tight-lipped/banished/sparked) about it.

11. Anna's parents are quite ᵃ(wary/mugged/turned around/deterred) of what she has got herself into in dating this odd bloke. Her trouble is that she ᵇ(sparks/knee-jerks/mopes/craves) male affection, especially from dodgy guys like him.

12: ᵃ(Spark/Mope/Overlook/Banish)any thought of going into the acting profession. It's a ᵇ(mug's game/backlash/blunder/heyday).

13. If we want to be at the ᵃ(farce/gulf/cutting edge/wake) of modern education, we have no choice but to ᵇ(banish/opt out of/mug up/crave) the local school authority.

14. It was a ᵃ(blundering/farcical/gruelling/overlooking) afternoon of tough negotiating, but at least it has now ᵇ(sparked/craved/turned around/plugged) debate about the major issues we need to address.

15. A: I have made up my mind and I won't be ᵃ(turned around/overlooked/deterred/mugged) by you or anybody else.
B: OK. That's fine, but I just don't want whatever you decide to be a ᵇ(gruelling/tight-lipped/ moping/knee-jerk) response, not properly thought out.

Chapter Two

Lesson One

Stark (Complete, absolute--*note that "stark" cannot be used in every sense of the word complete. One could not say, for example, "He is a stark idiot." It is most commonly found with "contrast" or "reality", as in the examples below*.)

Examples:
- There was a **stark** contrast between the two patients. One was moping around feeling sorry for himself, while the other had managed to turn his life around.
- The **stark** reality is that we are no longer at the cutting edge of modern technology.

To bicker (To argue in a bad-tempered way about unimportant things--*usually with someone with whom one has a close relationship*)

Examples:
- Overall, the kids get on well, but on occasions they do **bicker**. That's when I have to banish them to their rooms.
- My mum and dad were always **bickering** over something silly. This caused a series of much nastier rows, leading to their eventual divorce. Great shame.

In the limelight (The focus of public attention)

Examples:
- In his heyday he was always **in the limelight**. Now he likes to keep a low profile.
- At the time, the blunders she made as Foreign Secretary put her **in the limelight** more than she would have liked. But now she's trying to plug her autobiography, they'll stand her in good stead.

To be seething (To be furiously angry)

Examples:
- She had no right to give me such a dressing down in front of my colleagues. I was absolutely **seething** afterwards.
- I could see him in the corner, **seething** as the interviewer gave his wife a gruelling time with some tough questions. But that's what happens if you put your family in the limelight.

Underhand (Deceptive, dishonest--*used to describe an action, often secretive, rather than a person*)

Examples:
- *He has the gift of the gab, so I was a bit wary of him, but as it turned out, nothing **underhand** had happened. Not this time, anyway.*
- *I'm not a mug, you know. I'm sure you're up to no good. Something **underhand** is going on, I'm certain of it.*

All hell broke loose (Everything went crazy/out of control)

Examples:
- *The authorities tried to deter people from turning out to see the new Princess arrive at Buckingham Palace, but as soon as she got out of the royal car, **all hell broke loose.***
- *In the wake of his recent release from prison, **all hell broke loose** amongst his followers. However, the fact that some people love him and every stupid thing he says doesn't mean that he's going to be able to turn his life around.*

To turn a blind eye to/towards (To pretend not to notice that something negative is happening)

Examples:
- *Even if you're seething with anger, it's better that you **turn a blind eye to** what is going on. Opting for a quiet life is always the best policy.*
- *Her husband is beginning to lose his marbles, but she **turns a blind eye towards** it and tries to banish the thought of not being able to cope.*

To burden, a burden (To cause inconvenience, to disturb; an inconvenience)

Examples:
- *I'm so sorry to **burden** you with my problems, but in the light of what has happened, I don't think I can just turn a blind eye, do you?*
- *The heavy **burden** of having to take on unqualified staff during the Christmas period is one we cannot afford to overlook.*

To mellow, mellow (To become more relaxed and easy-going--*especially as one gets older*-- quiet and relaxing--*especially music or a person's character*)

Examples:
- *I think my father and I have only bonded relatively recently because he has begun to **mellow** in his old age. We have stopped bickering and he is no longer constantly seething with rage. This is in stark contrast to earlier years.*
- *Can you put on something **mellow** like a Chopin Prelude? I'm feeling rather shattered after a gruelling week.*

Tantrum (A burst of anger, screaming and shouting-- *usually from a young child, baby or an adult behaving like a child*)

Examples:
- *As you know, my young child is prone to having **tantrums** in the middle of a supermarket. That's why I don't like to burden my parents with him when they go shopping.*
- *The boss is having one of her **tantrums**. I don't think now is the right time to accuse her of doing something underhand; all hell will break loose.*

*"I'm not a mug, you know. I'm sure you're up to no good. Something **underhand** is going on, I'm certain of it".*

(see page 16)

Lesson Two

To flatter (To pay someone a compliment--*often in order to gain some benefit. Note that "to be flattered" means to feel honoured and pleased. See example 2. Also note the expression "flattery will get you nowhere", which means that being nice to someone will not necessarily get you what you want. It is generally used in a light-hearted, informal manner.*)

Examples:
- *He's always trying to **flatter** his female clients, speaking to them with that smooth, mellow voice of his. He thinks he's got the gift of the gab.*
- *She **was flattered** by all the attention she received. This was in stark contrast to last year when she was banished from the limelight by the media, who were more interested in her daughter.*
- *I'm very wary of pretentious people who haven't actually read my books trying to plug them and saying cringingly nice things about me. **Flattery will get them nowhere**.*

To stifle, stifling (To prevent, suppress or constrain an activity or idea; to restrict one's freedom; suffocating)

Examples:
- *I feel that the Government's actions have been underhand. They are clearly trying to **stifle** debate on the issue.*
- A: *I have an inexplicable craving for hot chocolate.*
- B: *In this **stifling** heat?*

To strive (To try with difficulty; to make a great effort to achieve something--*very often used with "for"*)

Examples:
- *If we want to **strive** <u>for</u> a decent society, we will have to step up our efforts to improve the standard of education for the poor in this country.*
- *The Indians and Pakistanis are still **striving** <u>for</u> peace, although they are very wary of each other.*

To be dismayed (To be very disappointed/shocked by an action or decision)

Examples:
- We **were** somewhat **dismayed** when we discovered that our son's school had opted out of the council-run literacy programme for local schools. His teacher told us it was because the programme could stifle the children's love of literature. Oh please!
- After all she had striven for, she **was dismayed** at the new president's decision to turn a blind eye to the previous government's human rights abuses.

Busybody (Someone who interferes with/organises other people's affairs without being asked to do so--*a negative expression*)

Examples:
- She says that she doesn't like to burden people with her own problems, but when it comes to the lives of others, she's a real **busybody**. Someone needs to give her a dressing-down.
- If you hadn't been such a **busybody** trying to organise her life, she wouldn't now be having so many tantrums. And just at a time when she was showing signs of mellowing.

To brace oneself for something (To prepare oneself for bad news/something unpleasant)

Examples:
- Before you meet my parents, I'd better warn you that they never stop bickering…and my dad's losing his marbles. So, **brace yourself**!
- She told me that it was no good turning a blind eye to all the goings-on at work, and that I should **brace myself** for a hectic few weeks ahead when all hell is likely to break loose.

To deploy (To position troops/weapons so that they can be used immediately)

Examples:
- The stark reality with which all of us must come to terms is that enemy forces have **deployed** missiles and bombs in strategic locations around the city.
- A: It is so boring having to listen to politicians go on and on about the "need" to **deploy** more troops in Afghanistan.

  B: Oh yes indeed; I was trying to stifle a yawn too.

Vulnerable (In a position where one can easily get hurt--*either physically or emotionally*--; weak and without protection)

Examples:
- *Unless we take the bull by the horns, we will be leaving ourselves in an increasingly **vulnerable** position.*
- *You can't overlook the fact that he was feeling extremely **vulnerable** in the wake of that farce involving his father's business dealings.*

To deplete, depleted (To use up the supply/resources of something; no longer in sufficient supply)

Examples:
- *Environmentalists have complained that excessive fishing of cod in the seas surrounding the UK has dramatically **depleted** stocks, and they are dismayed that the powers that be are turning a blind eye to this state of affairs.*
- *The number of maths teachers in our school is seriously **depleted**. We are going to have to step up recruitment if we want to remain at the cutting edge of education in this city.*

To mourn, be in mourning (To show how sad one is because of someone's death or because one has lost the use or benefit of something which had previously brought pleasure; to be in a state of sorrow following a death)

Examples:
- *She will remain in this vulnerable state until she stops **mourning** for her mother, who passed away nearly two years ago. She needs to brace herself for a life without her, sad though that is.*
- *The whole school still **mourns** the loss of its playing fields just at a time when many of the pupils were striving for success in their chosen sports.*
- *She **was in mourning** for her late husband until she had the pleasure and joy of becoming a grandmother. That certainly turned her life around.*

"The number of maths teachers in our school is seriously **depleted**. We are going to have to step up recruitment if we want to remain at the cutting edge of education in this city." (see page 20)

Lesson Three

To be outlawed (To be made illegal--*note that an "**outlaw**" is a rather dated term for a criminal who is hiding from the police. See 3rd example below.*)

Examples:
- The underhand practices of many multinational companies have now, thankfully, been **outlawed**.
- In stark contrast to the custom in some European countries, smoking in public places has been **outlawed** in most U.S. states.
- We will turn a blind eye to those families who have been housing **outlaws**, providing they own up immediately.

Fat cat (A very highly paid person, often an industrialist or company director, who is usually considered not to be worth the money he is paid--*a negative expression*)

Examples:
- I think the future of some of the **fat cats** running the railways is doomed. I certainly won't mourn any of them if they go.
- As a **fat cat** of the country's largest gas energy provider, he has allowed supplies to become depleted while continuing to pay himself a huge company dividend. This is corruption and should be outlawed.

To lure, lure (To attract someone to a particular place or activity; the appeal/attraction of something)

Examples:
- The beautiful beaches, sunshine and laid-back lifestyle **lured** me to the Caribbean. I'd had quite enough of the gruelling routine of London.
- I am bracing myself for a very bad year…and the thought of doing something a lot less stressful, like writing cookery books, is **luring** me away from the restaurant business.
- The **lure** of the dollar is what attracts so many international companies to the United States. But they are all striving for the same thing and competition is fierce.

Glum (Sad and full of despair)

Examples:
- I don't know why you look so **glum**. I'd be quite flattered if people had been so complimentary about my work.
- She looks like she's in mourning for someone, all dressed in black. Is she always so **glum**?

To overhaul, overhaul (To examine and change a system; a major change to a system)

Examples:
- We must be careful not to allow ourselves to be lured into the expensive exercise of **overhauling** our computer system. It's very easy for fat cats to keep telling us we need to spend money.
- There has to be a total **overhaul** of the National Health Service before the image of a Third World country can be banished from our minds.

Spate (A series of events happening over a short period of time--*usually something negative*)

Examples:
- There has been a **spate** of robberies here over the last few weeks. This area is fast becoming renowned as a haven for outlaws.
- We've had a **spate** of cases recently where vulnerable women have been sexually exploited by criminal gangs. Police investigations of this serious problem need to be stepped up.

Cover-up (A hiding of the truth about a mistake or crime)

Examples:
- An overhaul of the medical profession could help to prevent **cover-ups** when mistakes have been made.
- The whole thing has been a massive **cover-up**. Now the truth has come to light, all hell will break loose..

To be poised to do something (To be ready for action)

Examples:
- They were **poised to** attack the enemy. Unfortunately, they didn't realise at the time that their own military resources were severely depleted.

- It's a refreshing change to see such a seemingly mellow guy **poised to** take over as lead vocalist of the country's loudest heavy metal band.

"They were **poised to** attack the enemy. Unfortunately, they didn't realise at the time that their own military resources were severely depleted." (see page 23).

Feat (An accomplishment, achievement--*note the expression* **"no mean feat"**, *which means not easy to do, and therefore quite an achievement*)

Examples:
- The cover-ups surrounding this loss-making project were a major **feat** in themselves and must have taken a lot of intricate planning.
- Being able to handle my child's tantrums is a **feat** I'm still striving to achieve.

- A: *Your wife talks even more than mine, and that's **no mean feat**, I can tell you.*
  B: *She will be flattered to hear that. I'll let her know.*

To be renowned for something (To be well known for something)

Examples:
- *You'd better brace yourself for some strong weather. This island **is renowned for** its hurricanes.*
- *I'd be very wary of him if I were you; he's **renowned for** his tantrums and he tends to lose the plot.*

NEWS BULLETIN

Last night MP (Member of Parliament) Peter Miller was seething with anger after being accused of having masterminded a spate of cover-ups concerning business interests he is alleged to have in various American multinationals. Mr Miller, generally known as quite a mellow character, got embroiled in some fiery bickering with members of the Opposition in the House of Commons today. He assured the House that nothing underhand was going on and that the idea that he was becoming renowned as a fat cat left him somewhat hurt and dismayed. He was seen leaving Westminster looking rather glum, which was in stark contrast to his mood last week when he was poised to become the new Secretary for Overseas Trade.

In other news, in the Middle East, Israel has deployed more troops on the West Bank in light of the fact that several Jewish settlers have recently been lured to their deaths by Palestinian rebels posing as United Nations peacekeepers. A spokesman for the Israeli government said that military protection in the area had become depleted in recent months, leaving its citizens vulnerable to attack.

Meanwhile several Palestinian families were still in mourning over the death of five children killed in recent Israeli air raids. Both sides are bracing themselves for further violence.

MAN AND WOMAN ON A BLIND DATE

MONICA: *You must be Tony? I'm sorry if I've kept you waiting. I'm Monica.*

TONY: *Hi! Don't worry, it's no problem. I must say, I didn't expect you to be so beautiful.*

MONICA: *Flattery will get you nowhere, I have to warn you! I'm not usually late, by the way…and sorry to burden you with my personal life on our first date, but I've been striving to sort out a few problems at work.*

TONY: *Oh that's a feat I've been trying to achieve for twenty years.*

MONICA: *Well, I'm in charge of about fifteen office workers and one of them is a real busybody. For a long time I've turned a blind eye to her interfering ways, but today she had a tantrum when I suggested she should get on with her own work and not try to seize the limelight at every opportunity. I can tell you all hell broke loose. She lost it completely…*

TONY: *(Desperate to escape) Oh…Wait a minute. I think someone's trying to call me on my mobile…I'll be back in a minute.*

Chapter Two: **Exercise**

CHOOSE THE CORRECT WORD FROM THOSE IN GREEN
Answers on page 139

1. *You know, working in this* ^a*(stark/bickering/stifling/baffling) heat makes me realise that the air conditioning in this office needs to be completely* ^b*(overhauled/outlawed/depleted/deployed).*

2. *London Underground passengers have been advised by the media to* ^a*(burden/deplete/lure/brace) themselves for a* ^b*(cover-up/spate/feat/tantrum) of one-day strikes.*

3. *She is becoming* ^a*(glum/renowned/lured/vulnerable) for her* ^b*(flattery/tantrums/seething/feats). My colleagues try to* ^c*(turn a blind eye/mourn/deploy/bicker) to her immature behaviour, but I think her outbursts are uncalled for.*

4. *It's almost a year since his death, but his wife is still* ^a*(depleted/glum/in the limelight/in mourning). I miss him myself. He was such a lovely,* ^b*(outlawed/flattering/mellow/underhand) sort of guy.*

5. ^a*After a day of having to listen to my kids* ^a*(bickering/seething/turning a blind eye/bracing themselves), my energy levels feel completely* ^b*(underhand/renowned/overhauled/depleted).*

6. *The thing is, I know she's feeling particularly* ^a*(depleted/vulnerable/dismayed/like a busybody) during this difficult period of her life, and I don't want to* ^b*(burden/bicker/lure/overhaul) her with my own problems.*

7. *I felt really* ^a*(vulnerable/burdened/flattered/stifled) when the boss told me that achieving my sales target so early on in the year was a tremendous* ^b*(feat/spate/fat cat/cover-up).*

8. ^a*(Striving/Seething/Stifling/Poising) to do better than her peers is in* ^b*(mellow/stark/glum/depleted) contrast to how she was as a shy, withdrawn teenager. Now she is happy to be* ^c*(underhand/flattered/a busybody/in the limelight).*

9. *All* ^a*(tantrums came out/stocks were depleted/hell broke loose/fat cats were destroyed) when Alison found out what Gavin had been up to. She was* ^b*(deployed/seething/bickering/mourning).*

10. *For these* ^a*(fat cats/flatterers/busybodies/mellow guys) to get so rich, they have to be doing something* ^b*(depleted/vulnerable/underhand/renowned).*

11. ^a*(Seething/Mourning/Deploying/Stifling) nuclear missiles so near a thriving, young community should be* ^b*(outlawed/overhauled/covered up/turned a blind eye).*

12. *I was* ^a*(dismayed/renowned/stifled/flattered) to discover that the* ^b*(deployment/tantrum/limelight/lure) of a better life in Australia had made him leave his family.*

13.   *She was* ^a*(outlawed/poised/seething/flattered) to relate to everyone what she had overheard in the ladies' toilets, but then she remembered that her husband had always told her not to be a* ^b*(busybody/fat cat/bickerer/spate).*

14.   *We were all looking rather* ^a*(depleted/glum/renowned/stark) when we realised what trouble we had got ourselves into. I was wondering whether there was any way we could subtly organise a* ^b*(mourning/busybody/cover-up/flattery).*

Lesson One

To take its toll on (To have a lasting, damaging effect on someone/something)

Examples:
- The latest spate of redundancies has **taken its toll on** the workforce.
- The stifling heat of this city is beginning to **take its toll on** all of us. I never thought I would mourn English winters.

To be stunned, stunning (To be shocked/amazed; amazing, extremely beautiful)

Examples:
- Even though we had braced ourselves for a gruelling dressing-down, we were **stunned** by the severity of his words.
- She was somewhat **stunned** by his unwarranted flattery. It was a bit over the top.
- I was lured by her **stunning** smile. She has since become renowned for this.

Fake (Unreal, false, not genuine)

Examples:
- Allegedly, he used a **fake** passport to get into the country, but the police are quite hopeful of avoiding any further blunders.
- It's true he has the gift of the gab, but it's a cover-up. Everyone knows deep down he is a complete **fake**.

To reimburse (To pay back money to someone--*often used for expenses*)

Examples:
- He has sat moping in his room all day just because his manager has refused to **reimburse** him for his monthly travel card. Pathetic!
- We have opted for plan B because it will be easier to **reimburse** committee members for the expenses they incur.

Hard-line, hard-liner (A strict and uncompromising view on something; a person who rigidly sticks to a set of ideas--*i.e. not a moderate; very often a politician*)

Examples:
- The school's Board of Governors will take a **hard-line** on teachers who fail to come up to scratch. They are poised to make a few recommendations, I hear.
- The new socialist government have adopted a **hard-line** approach towards fat cats, despite the fact that in the past many of these hypocritical politicians have craved their financial sponsorship.
- We have striven to create a political climate in which moderates feel free to mingle with **hard-liners.**

To set in (To give the appearance of being permanent--*usually something unpleasant and often used with cold weather or winter*)

Examples:
- The cold weather has unfortunately taken its toll on the old people of the village. Winter is definitely **setting in**.
- As infection had already **set in**, saving the patient's life was a stunning feat on the part of the surgeon.

To step in (To intervene and take action)

Examples:
- The police will have to **step in** if they want to stave off civil unrest. And a lot of shopkeepers will need reimbursing after this current spate of shoplifting.
- I've got a bee in my bonnet about bad grammar and that's why I had to **step in** and talk to Daniel's English teacher. But I was stunned to discover that her grammar was even worse than his.

To rally round (To support someone in times of difficulty)

Examples:
- No wonder he's looking glum: in hindsight, we should have **rallied round** him when she first accused him of sponging off her parents. What a nasty woman she is.
- A: Even though their recent performances have left a lot to be desired, we all ought to **rally round** the team, who, on paper at least, could win the title.

  B: Not unless the Chairman steps in and appoints a new manager.

To make a killing (To make a lot of money easily and quickly)

Examples:

- A: *My accountant assured me that we are poised to **make a killing** with our new line in ladies' lingerie. That will be no mean feat in today's market. I'm not sure he's right.*
  B: *Stop doing yourselves down. Other businesses might be doomed; not yours!*
- *Plenty of companies **made a killing** on the internet last year, but the demise of so many of them has sparked furious debate amongst economists.*

*"The cold weather has unfortunately taken its toll on the old people of the village. Winter is definitely **setting in**."*

(see page 30)

Lesson Two

To implement (To put into practice, to carry out--*especially a plan or law*)

Examples:
- *If the Government don't step in and **implement** some of the policies they set out in their manifesto before the last election, they will be heavily criticised by the hard-liners in the party.*
- *I don't know if anyone realises, but when the council **implement** this new planning law, many property owners will have to be reimbursed.*

To deplore, deplorable (To disapprove/condemn strongly; deserving condemnation, extremely bad)

Examples:
- *We all **deplore** the cumbersome way in which complaints are dealt with in the National Health Service. The whole system needs overhauling.*
- *Most doctors **deplore** the lack of support from the Government. That's why they are being lured overseas.*
- *It's **deplorable** that these guys have been allowed to make a killing by exploiting vulnerable old people.*

To gather pace/momentum (To speed up, go faster)

Examples:
- *I must admit, as the Republican Party's election campaign **gathers pace**, the idea of the Democrats having another term in office is growing on me.*
- *I was just thinking about the gulf in class between our rail service, not renowned for its speed, and those operated in France and Germany, when suddenly the train I was on began to **gather momentum**... but only for a few seconds. We got stuck in a tunnel soon afterwards.*

Livelihood (Something that provides a person with money or other means to support themselves--*usually a job or whatever one does to survive on a daily basis*)

Examples:
- *I'm in constant fear of losing my **livelihood**, especially if all the Government cutbacks are implemented.*

- *I'm still utterly stunned that writing has provided me with a **livelihood**. My dad told me it was a mug's game and I should just get a proper job.*

Vindictive (Nasty, unpleasant and hurtful)

Examples:
- A: *I'm not trying to be **vindictive**, but your company can hardly be said to be at the cutting-edge of technology.*
- B: *Well, it provides over 15,000 people with a livelihood, but then I wouldn't expect that to be of any importance to someone like you. Not exactly renowned as a journalist who looks into things too deeply, are you Jim?*
- *The **vindictive** attack she launched on my family was deplorable. Luckily we have enough friends who rallied around us.*

To go with the flow (To see how things turn out; to follow one's instinct and see how things go)

Examples:
- A: *You should turn a blind eye to all the bickering that goes on between you. For the time being, I think you should just go **with the flow**.*
- B: *That will be a disaster. I can't fake happiness.*
- *Instead of feeling glum about the future, why don't you just **go with the flow**? You might be unnecessarily bracing yourself for something that will never happen.*

Downfall (A cause of sudden ruin, loss of wealth/reputation)

Examples:
- *I think it was just a knee-jerk reaction, but it proved to be his **downfall**. He should have kept tight-lipped about it.*
- *Our **downfall** was that we didn't go with the flow when events started to gather pace, don't you think?*

*"Our **downfall** was that we didn't go with the flow when events started to gather pace, don't you think?"* (see page 33)

To flog a dead horse (To try to make something succeed when it is too late because it has already failed, and therefore is a pointless action)

Examples:
- *Trying to win the Championship with these players is a feat that can never be achieved. It's like we're **flogging a dead horse**.*
- *The teething problems we had should have warned us what we were letting ourselves in for. Really, we're just **flogging a dead horse** trying to revive this business…unless some fat cat benefactor steps in.*

Lesson Three

To resort to (To be forced to do something unpleasant when no other course of action could be taken--*note also the expression "as a last resort", which means something has been/will be done only when there is no other choice*)

Examples:
- A: *He said he only **resorted to** violence because he was pushed into doing so.*

  B: *That's rubbish. I've known him since he was a boy. He's a nasty, vindictive yob.*
- *We really need to start implementing the policies we agreed at last month's meeting; otherwise we might have to **resort** to redundancies.*
- *I'm very wary of these fast-food places. I'll only go there **as a last resort**.*

"Rather you/him than me!" ("I don't envy you/him at all"; "I'm glad it's not me having to do that")

Examples:
- A: *I'm going to have to talk to her about her tantrums. She can't continue to get away with them.*

  B: ***Rather you than me!** I'll be stunned if she listens to a word you say.*
- A: *I've been led to believe that Jane Smith is a bit of a hard-liner. She'll be taking over as CEO in June.*

  B: ***Rather her than me!** The company is finished. No point in flogging a dead horse.*

In tatters (Ruined, destroyed, in a bad state)

Examples:
- *Once the cold weather had set in, we realised that our plans for a picnic in the country were **in tatters**.*
- *His confidence is **in tatters** after the Head Teacher asked him to step down as Deputy Head. We should all rally round him in his hour of need.*

"It's/He's not my cup of tea" ("It's/He's not the sort of thing I like")

Examples:

- That picture is almost certainly a fake. Anyway, **it's not really my cup of tea**.
- A: I wouldn't go out with him, even as a last resort. He's not my cup of tea at all.

  B: Am I your cup of tea?

  A: Yuk!

To clinch (To settle definitely and conclusively; to get a good result after much difficulty--usually at the last minute)

Examples:

- Playing too defensively was the home team's downfall, and perhaps not surprisingly the visitors **clinched** victory in the dying seconds of the game.
- We hope to **clinch** the deal on Friday afternoon…and make a killing by the end of the month.

To stick to one's guns (To insist one is right; not to give up or change one's opinion or attitude)

Examples:

- If I've got a bee in my bonnet about something, I will **stick to my guns** and not let any busybody try and influence me.
- Sometimes by **sticking to one's guns** at all costs instead of going with the flow, one can find oneself to be out of one's depth.

Commiserations (Sympathy, "I feel sorry for you")

Examples:

- A: **Commiserations**! I really thought you were going to clinch a result in the last minute.

  B: But we didn't…and now our season is in tatters.
- We'd like to offer our **commiserations**, but remain hopeful that you will get into a good university.

To wreak havoc (To cause a lot of chaos/disorder--*note also the expression "**to wreak revenge on**", which means to get one's revenge on someone*)

Examples:
- *A number of young drunk men have **wreaked havoc** on this small town, smashing up shops and carrying out a spate of muggings. There will be a backlash from the community.*
- *By half time they knew they were flogging a dead horse. The opposition's main striker was **wreaking havoc** with their defence.*
- *He is trying to **wreak revenge on** the directors of this company for ruining his livelihood.*

A: "I wouldn't go out with him, even as a last resort. He's not my cup of tea at all.
B: Am I your cup of tea?
A: Yuk!"

(see page 36)

To chip in

i. (To help pay for something; to contribute money for a particular purpose)
Examples:
- *He's renowned for sponging off his friends. He knows they'll **chip in** whenever his finances are in tatters.*
- *We'd be happy to **chip in** if you need money for a holiday, but keep tight-lipped about it. Don't tell your brother.*

ii. (To join in a conversation by making a comment)
Examples:
- A: *He's always poised to **chip in** on any conversation concerning restaurants in London.*
- B: *...which is a great pity because he rarely knows what he's talking about. Most of the places he raves over are not my cup of tea.*
- *My gut reaction was to **chip in** and ask to be reimbursed immediately, but I know speaking out usually proves to be my downfall, so I kept my mouth shut.*

Heads will/would (etc.) roll (People at the top of the company/organisation will lose their jobs)

Examples:
- A: *The whole board of directors is responsible for this cover-up. Heads will definitely roll.*
- B: *I bet they won't. They'll all stick to their guns and protest their innocence. You'll see.*
- *I think if they hadn't clinched that agreement, heads would have **begun to roll.***

CONVERSATION BETWEEN TWO GENERAL PRACTITIONERS (GPS OR FAMILY DOCTORS)

JOHN: *You know this week has really taken its toll on me. I'm exhausted.*

DAVID: *Me too! Just trying to keep up with paperwork wreaks havoc on my social life.*

JOHN: *Social life? Is that what you call it? Mine's in absolute tatters. I can't remember the last time I had a night out with friends.*

DAVID: *It's all the bureaucracy and targets forced on us by the Government. The patients suffer in the end. If only the Health Secretary would listen to the very reasonable suggestions of GPs. But it's like flogging a dead horse. The politicians will just stick to their guns and ignore us.*

JOHN: *They will indeed. Actually, my cousin Janet, who is also a GP, has had to resort to opting out of the NHS (National Health Service). Now she's making a killing in the private sector.*

DAVID: *Good for her. I think I might do the same. I felt like doing just that the other day when I read about the Local Authority's mean offer to reimburse us just £10.00 for making medical reports for insurance companies. I was stunned by that.*

JOHN: *Oh nothing surprises me anymore. I know everyone working in the public sector is complaining about cutbacks and low wages, but I really do think our livelihoods are at stake, and that if the Health Secretary's latest proposals to revolutionise GP practices are implemented, it will lead to the downfall of our profession.*

DAVID: *You're making me feel depressed. Wouldn't it be great if the Health Secretary were to step down...or even fall under a bus?*

JOHN: *Now you're being vindictive. Do you honestly believe we would be able to clinch some amazing agreement with his successor or any other politician? I can't even imagine the general public rallying round their local GPs. They think we're all like fat cat businessmen.*

DAVID: *I wish!*

Saturday afternoon, I was glued to the radio as usual, half expecting the inevitable. And indeed, Arsenal, my team since I was seven years old, threw away a lead and lost the game. Typical! My sister offered her commiserations, but I was inconsolable. I think heads should roll at my club if results don't start improving.

In the evening my mother told me she was going to a meeting at the local vegetarian society. "Rather you than me!" I sympathised. As she made her way to the front door, I noticed she was wearing what I thought was a white fox fur coat. My reproving glance invited a prompt response: "Don't worry, it's a fake. You know very well that real fur coats aren't my cup of tea." My sister chipped in with: "Even giving the impression you are wearing a dead animal is deplorable, especially if you are going to meet vegetarians. What message are you giving out? I, on the other hand, don't even wear leather… Well, only as a last resort.". I had to step in. "Mum, don't listen to her; you look stunning…if you like foxes". She took one look back at us as she exited and uttered, "What pretentious children I have. Hypocrites!"

On Sunday evening I was striving to meet deadlines for my homework. And exam preparations are now gathering pace. I mustn't allow a state of panic to set in. Maybe I should be like my sister and just go with the flow. It never did her any harm.

What an exciting life I lead!

Chapter Three: **Exercise**

CHOOSE THE CORRECT WORD FROM THOSE IN GREEN
Answers on page 139

1. The Prime Minister had to ª(*flog a dead horse/step in/clinch/set in*) in order to prevent the ᵇ(*deplorables/fakes/tatters/hard-liners*) in Parliament from getting their own way.

2. It's incredible what can happen in a short space of time. Last year they made a ª(*resort/ downfall/killing/livelihood*), and now the business is in ᵇ(*tatters/commiserations/havoc/flow*).

3. His wife's death has certainly taken ª(*its toll/a hard line/commiserations/reimbursement*) on him, but his family has ᵇ(*flogged a dead horse/set in/resorted to violence/rallied round*) despite also being ᶜ(*deplored/chipped/in tatters/stunned*) by the suddenness of it.

4. I don't want to sound ª(*faked/in tatters/vindictive/deplorable*), but your boyfriend is not ᵇ(*my cup of tea/a hard-liner/a dead horse/my downfall*).

5. The new regulations about provision of discounted central heating for the old have to be ª(*reimbursed/clinched/stunned/implemented*) before the cold weather ᵇ(*chips in/rallies round/sets in/goes with the flow*). The winters always ᶜ(*wreak havoc/step in/stick to their guns/clinch*) on their health and mobility.

6. A: ª(*Downfall/Commiserations/Dead horses/Tatters*) for not winning the contract.
    B: Yes, it is a shame, especially as negotiations were ᵇ(*gathering momentum/rallying round/ being clinched/sticking to their guns*). Anyway, as the clients are going to ᶜ(*make a killing/be stunned/wreak havoc/reimburse*) us for the expenses we incurred, I shan't lose any sleep over it.

7. His ª(*downfall/commiserations/implementations/livelihood*) was that he made up his mind too early instead of just ᵇ(*flogging a dead horse/resorting to violence/going with the flow/ rallying round*). The matter is now closed, so there is no point in ᶜ(*making a killing/flogging a dead horse/wreaking havoc/being vindictive*).

8. I ª(*fake/clinch/deplore/flog*) begging on the streets and I would only do it myself as a ᵇ(*downfall/hardliner/last resort/revenge*).

9. A: I'm going to have to ask him to ª(*step down/chip in/rally round/set in*) as chairman of the committee. I'm not looking forward to it.
    B: ᵇ(*Heads will roll/Rather you than me/Commiserations/ He's not my cup of tea*)!

10. If they don't ª(*reimburse/step in/implement/clinch*) a deal with one of the big investment banks, ᵇ(*they will stick to their guns/heads will roll/they will make a killing/it will take its toll*).

11. A: *He can't afford to stop teaching; it's his main* ᵃ(*fake/momentum/downfall/livelihood*).
B: *Well, I'm happy to* ᵇ(*chip in/rally round/gather pace/wreak havoc*) *if it can help him make ends meet.*

12. *If you believe in something, you have to* ᵃ(*flog a dead horse/stick to your guns/step down/ step in*). *In the end, people will respect you for it. Much better than being a* ᵇ(*havoc/ hardliner/fake/cup of tea*).

Chapter Four

Lesson One

To be set in one's ways (Not to like change as one gets older; to have fixed ideas and habits)

Examples:
- He thinks that a steady relationship with someone will wreak havoc on his social life. He has become too **set in his ways**.
- My dad is really **set in his ways**. Getting him to change is like flogging a dead horse.

A godsend (A piece of unexpected good luck that arrives at the right moment)

Examples:
- My grandfather's offering to chip in was an absolute **godsend**; otherwise I would have had to resort to asking my mother-in-law for money again.
- In hindsight, my being asked to step down was a **godsend**. Retirement has turned my life around.

To bowl over (To impress someone significantly)

Examples:
- A: I must say, she completely **bowled me over** as soon as I set eyes upon her.
  B: Really? She's not my cup of tea at all.
- I was **bowled over** by his book. It really is at the cutting edge of modern fiction. I've read such rubbish recently; this book was a godsend.

A fad (A temporary fashion)

Examples:
- It's quite normal for teenagers to be bowled over by current **fads**.
- Going to work on a scooter is his latest **fad**. I'm sure he's losing his marbles.

*"Going to work on a scooter is his latest **fad**. I'm sure he's losing his marbles."*
(see page 43)

To take liberties (To do something one should not do, knowing or hoping that one will get away with it--*see Practical Everyday English, page 78*--; to be too familiar with someone--*note the expression **"to take the liberty of doing something"**, which is used when someone has dared to do something without first asking permission*)

Example:
- *He knows that the company's proposed new policy of making all male employees wear a tie is unlikely to be implemented, but I do think he's **taking liberties** coming to the office in jeans. Don't you?*
- *Don't **take liberties** with me, young man. Flattery will get you nowhere.*
- A: ***I took the liberty** of using your rubbish bin, as mine was full. I hope you don't mind.*
- B: *That's no problem at all. I only wish that in this stifling heat the bins were emptied more often than once a week.*

To plod on/through (To continue at a slow pace; to work slowly at something boring--*note that a "**plodder**" is someone who goes through life or school at a slow pace, but never gives up*)

Example:
- *Initially I thought that my work on the contract was gathering pace, but now I can see that I will just have **to plod on** with it until I get it done.*
- *I tell you what: **plodding through** this dull text book is a feat I might not be able to complete. I'm not exactly bowled over by the subject matter or the style in which it is written.*
- *There's a gulf of difference between my two boys; David is the sort of boy who will take the bull by the horns, but Peter, on the other hand, is one of life's **plodders**. He'll get there in the end, but it will be a long road.*

Palaver (A lot of fuss, chaos and confusion--*not generally used for very serious situations such as a tragic accident*)

Example:
- *I hadn't properly braced myself for the **palaver** at the bank yesterday. I could have done without it.*
- *She doesn't want to go through all that **palaver** again. It has already taken its toll on her.*

On tenterhooks (Uncertain and anxious about what is going to happen in the near future)

Examples:
- *We were all **on tenterhooks** waiting to hear who had been promoted, but the boss just plodded on endlessly with what he was doing. In the end I took the liberty of interrupting him and asking him directly.*
- *The interviewer kept me **on tenterhooks** right the way through the interview. It wreaked havoc with my nerves, I can tell you.*

To rope someone in/into (To persuade a reluctant person to join in an activity)

Examples:
- A: *I've been **roped in**to taking part in my daughter's Christmas play at school.*
- B: *Rather you than me!*

- He started attending discussion groups after work, and tried to **rope** me **in**; but I don't fancy getting myself involved in all that palaver.

To have a chip on one's shoulder (To feel, usually unjustly, that one has always been a victim)

Examples:
- He says that his life is in tatters since his divorce and, rather unreasonably, promises to wreak revenge on all women. He clearly has a big **chip on his shoulder.**
- Telling him to get rid of that **chip on his shoulder** is like flogging a dead horse. He will never accept that he's responsible for his own downfall.

Chapter Four

Lesson Two

Petty (Trivial/unimportant/not worth considering or arguing about; only concerned with unimportant things)

Examples:
- You may consider it a **petty** matter, but I happen to think heads should roll over this issue.
- A: Not only is he vindictive, but he's also renowned for being **petty**. Last week, for example, he almost had a tantrum when he caught an employee using company stationery for personal correspondence.

  B: Now that is **petty**, you're right.

To get on one's high horse (To respond angrily to someone/something in a superior or arrogant manner--*note also the expression "from the horse's mouth", which means from the person directly concerned or someone authoritative*)

Examples:
- There's no need to **get on your high horse** about it. I merely said that the music you listen to is not my cup of tea. That's all.
- If you take liberties with her, she's liable to **get on her high horse** and tell you that you're a "useless plodder". She said that to me once.
- A: Who told you to implement such a petty rule?

  B: I got it straight **from the horse's mouth**.

To reek of (To stink, smell awful--*note that a figurative use of "to reek" is to give a strong impression of an unpleasant quality or feature--see 3rd example below*)

Examples:
- He **reeked of** alcohol when he came to work this morning. His career and life are clearly in tatters, poor man.
- Your house, if you don't mind my saying, **reeks of** cats and dogs... and so I have taken the liberty of calling in specialist cleaners. Is that OK with you?
- There will be a backlash following on from the Prime Minister's speech to students last night. It **reeked of** hypocrisy.

To steal someone's thunder (To take the praise which someone else deserves rather than you; to be the centre of attention when it should have been someone else)

Examples:
- One can't overlook the fact that it was her idea. He **stole her thunder** simply because he has the gift of the gab.
- Her new dress designer has been a real godsend. In fact, she looked so good at the wedding that she even stole the bride's **thunder.**

"He **reeked of** alcohol when he came to work this morning. His career and life are clearly in tatters, poor man."
(see page 47)

48

To live up to (To prove equal to; to act in accordance with; to fulfil one's expectations- -*often used in the negative*)

Examples:
- *The show wasn't really my cup of tea at all. It <u>failed</u> **to live up to** all the hype. And it plodded on for over three hours. Torture!*
- *I'm <u>not</u> sure if the President will be able **to live up to** his promise to bridge the gulf between the two countries. His last state visit to France reeked of disorganisation.*

To ring a bell (To sound familiar)

Examples:
- A: *Now I can see what Sandra means: don't you remember her saying that Anna is always trying to steal her thunder?*

  B: *Now that you mention it, it does **ring a bell**, yes.*
- *She told me that he had made a killing on the Tokyo stock market, but his name doesn't **ring a bell** at all.*

To binge, a binge (To eat, drink or do some other pleasurable activity excessively; a short period of excessive eating, drinking etc.)

Examples:
- *Chocolate is my downfall. I can go for a week without it but then I tend to **binge**.*
- *He absolutely reeks of drink. I think he's been on one of his **binges** again. At one time I thought it was just a fad of his, but now I realise there is something more serious going on.*

To fob off (To appease someone/satisfy someone's enquiries, usually only temporarily, by deliberately giving them poor answers, excuses or something inferior)

Examples:
- *When he asked the minister if the law was likely to be implemented during this parliament, he was **fobbed off** with fake reassurances.*
- *I think we've managed to **fob them off** for the time being, but we'll have to brace ourselves for a more serious dressing-down in the weeks to come.*
- A: *I know it's taking liberties, but why don't you ask your boss for a pay rise?*

  B: *Because I know what he's like; he'll just try to **fob me off** with a new computer*

Shrewd (Clever, wise, keenly aware--*often used in a slightly negative sense*)

Examples:
- *I can tell you he's no mug. He's **shrewder** than he first appears and won't be fobbed off that easily.*
- *She invited herself on to the show so that she could plug her new book. A very **shrewd** move on her part.*

To have a field day (To take great pleasure in something, particularly in criticising something/someone in detail or at someone else's expense)

Examples:
- *Having to sit through that dreadful film was a gruelling experience for me. The critics are going to **have a field day** when it officially comes out in June.*
- A: *They **have** an absolute **field day** whenever I'm around, mocking all my weaknesses and failings.*

  B: *Someone sounds like they have a massive chip on their shoulder.*

Lesson Three

Easily led (Weak-willed; easily influenced by others--*used to describe a person who follows the behaviour and actions of stronger characters--a negative expression*)

Examples:
- School Report:
  Daniel is a bit of a "plodder" and needs to take the bull by the horns if he wants to do well in his exams next year. He should also be more assertive and not so **easily led** *by his classmates.*
- A: *I don't know how my daughter got into binge drinking.*
  B: *Too* **easily led** *by her peers, maybe?*

To bail out, bailout (To provide a large amount of financial assistance to an individual, business or country in order to save them from collapse; financial assistance to save from ruin)

Examples:
- *He went on a spending binge when he inherited a fortune from his grandfather. His shrewd wife, however, refused to* **bail him out** *when he was left with nothing. Sensible woman.*
- *Many members of the public are stunned that no heads have rolled at any of the banks which were in receipt of Government* **bailouts** *from the public purse. And they ask what regulations have been implemented to stop it happening again.*

To pull one's weight (To contribute one's fair share--*often used in the negative*)

Examples:
- *It certainly sparked debate when he accused some of the staff of <u>not</u>* **pulling their weight**.
- A: *If you ask me, marriage is a mug's game.*
  B: *You only say that because your husband <u>doesn't</u>* **pull his weight** *around the house.*
  A: *And he tries to fob me off with pathetic excuses like saying he has a bad back.*

To have one's work cut out for one (To have a lot of difficult work ahead; to have specific problems in the future which will need solving)

Example:
- *We really do **have our work cut out for us** here. It's not just a question of overhauling our software system.*
- *I don't think she realises what she has let herself in for. She's clearly got **her work cut out for her** this time, and no-one is going to bail her out if it all goes wrong.*

Not bat an eyelid/Without batting an eyelid (Not show/ Without showing concern, surprise, or any reaction)

Examples:
- *When the train started to go backwards, all hell broke loose amongst the passengers in our carriage, but Adrian **didn't bat an eyelid**. He just took it all in his stride.*

- A: *Even though the service left a lot to be desired, he paid the ludicrous bill **without batting an eyelid**.*
- B: *I would have made a fuss. Most restaurants in London don't live up to my expectations. Rip off!*

To bode well (To be a good sign for the future--*often used in the negative*)

Examples:
- *This spate of racial attacks does <u>not</u> **bode well** for the future. The police have their work cut out.*
- A: *Greece will definitely need bailing out.*
- B: *And who's next? It <u>doesn't</u> **bode well**, does it?*

To be out of the woods (To have overcome problems and difficulties)

Examples:
- A: *We're not **out of the woods** quite yet; we still have a few teething problems to sort out.*
- B: *I know…and the lure of retirement makes me wish we had never embarked on this venture in the first place.*
- Accountant:
  *You should be **out of the woods** by the summer. I have to say, though, that the way your last accountant prepared the tax papers was a farce.*

Client:
And you are a godsend, Michael. How would we cope without you?

Uplifting (Heartening, causing cheerfulness and high spirits--*often used to describe music and literature*)

Examples:
- *Mozart's piano sonatas are so spiritually **uplifting**…unlike the glum, depressing stuff you listen to.*
- A: *In the end, I'm pleased my husband roped me into going to see this play. It was a most **uplifting** production.*
  B: *I'm glad I got that information straight from the horse's mouth. Miriam told me you hated it.*

A: *"If you ask me, marriage is a mug's game.*
B: *You only say that because your husband <u>doesn't</u> **pull his weight** around the house.*
A: *And he tries to fob me off with pathetic excuses like saying he has a bad back."*
(see page 51)

Neck and neck (At the same level in a contest, election etc.)

Examples:
- It was **neck and neck** until the end of the season and then Real Madrid clinched the title from Barcelona on the last day.
- So far Boris Johnson and Ken Livingstone are **neck and neck** in the race to be the next London Mayor, and neither has resorted to dirty tactics…yet.

Underdog (A person or team not expected to win a game or competition)

Examples:
- Even though they had been written off as **underdogs**, they were poised for victory until the very last minute, when the favourites snatched a draw.
- A: He was sulking about having lost and it was no consolation to him that, as the **underdog**, nobody had expected him to win. He's desperate to wreak revenge on this opponent.

  B: That doesn't bode well at all. There is a gulf in class between them and that's why he lost and always will against this guy.

A PASSAGE FROM AN AUTOBIOGRAPHY

It's fair to say that when I was at school, I was quite easily led by the naughty boys. For my parents it made no difference that I was not generally one of the instigators of wrongdoing. I clearly did not live up to their expectations and I took liberties with them as well.

As I plodded on with my school work, my average marks did not bode well for the future. I definitely had my work cut out for me, but with some shrewd last-minute exam revision I managed to get into university; Cambridge, no less. During this time, I went through many fads, particularly with regard to my taste in music. In hindsight, I can now see that I had a bit of a chip on my shoulder about being the unfavoured younger brother. Peter was always a much more diligent student than I was, and I often attempted to steal his thunder when he came home with another academic success story. I tried to rope him into the rows I had with my parents about their not allowing me to be independent, but he didn't bat an eyelid.

And I must say that when I was waiting for my A level results, he was on tenterhooks just as much as I was. He was absolutely bowled over when I got into Cambridge…although those feelings of goodwill soon faded away when he had to bail me out after I spent nearly all of my student loan in just one term.

I love you, big brother!

STEVEN: *Although Manchester United and Arsenal are neck and neck, one has to say that Arsenal, having finished runners-up to United three years in a row, are still very much the underdogs. I seem to remember saying something similar three or four years ago. Do you remember?*

ANDREW: *It does ring a bell, yes. Anyway, it would be rather uplifting for the game and for neutral football fans if someone else won the title for a change. Don't you think?*

STEVEN: *I do. It would be a godsend. The Premier League has become far too predictable. We could do with some new champions. It would also be refreshing to see some younger managers; fresh faces. Most of the old ones have become set in their ways and get on their high horses whenever anyone has a go at them. They try to fob off the press by saying they don't want to become embroiled in petty arguments about how some of their players behave on and off the field.*

ANDREW: *Talking of fields, we're going to have a field day when this palaver about some of the Liverpool players going on regular drinking binges comes out. Apparently, even the captain often turns up for training reeking of booze.*

STEVEN: *Allegedly! But I don't think that's the main problem at Liverpool. It's more a case of too many players not pulling their weight.*

ANDREW: *Indeed. And this is precisely what is needed at the moment, when they're struggling to make the top half of the table. They're not out of the woods yet, are they?*

Chapter Four: **Exercise**

CHOOSE THE CORRECT WORD FROM THOSE IN GREEN
Answers on page 139

1. We should be ᵃ(*bowled over/out of the woods/fobbed off/on tenterhooks*) by December, and that's official. It came straight from ᵇ(*a field day/a godsend/the woods/the horse's mouth*).

2. The political journalists are going to have a ᵃ(*field day/bailout/binge/chip on their shoulder*) if this ᵇ(*liberty/shrewdness/palaver/bailout*) at Westminster continues.

3. In every match he is always branded the ᵃ(*godsend/underdog/thunder/palaver*). This is why he's got a ᵇ(*chip on his shoulder/bell to be rung/field day/fad*).

4. I told him that he had to ᵃ(*bat an eyelid/pull his weight/have a chip on his shoulder/bowl me over*), but he ᵇ(*took liberties/roped me in/fobbed me off/bailed out*) with some pathetic excuses about being under too much stress.

5. A: Don't you remember him? He was very ᵃ(*easily led/bowled over/on tenterhooks/plodding*) at school by the boys in the year above.
B: No, I'm sorry. His name doesn't ᵇ(*take liberties/bail me out/reek/ring a bell*) at all.

6. It's quite clear by her jealous actions that she wanted to ᵃ(*bat an eyelid/rope him in/steal his thunder/live up to him*), but he didn't even ᵇ(*bat an eyelid/rope her in/steal her thunder/live up to her*). It all seems rather ᶜ(*a palaver/petty/a godsend/a fad*) to me.

7. I thought that having such a great player at the club would be a ᵃ(*binge/fad/bailout/godsend*), but as it turns out, his tendency to make racist remarks about other players (and find them funny) does not ᵇ(*ring a bell/fob off/bode well/rope in*) for the future.

8. The film certainly ᵃ(*boded well/bowled over/lived up to/plodded on*) all its hype. I found it most ᵇ(*uplifting/plodding/bailed-out/petty*).

9. She has put on so much weight because she is prone to ᵃ(*bingeing/ringing a bell/flogging a dead horse/having a field day*). It's very sad. Her psychiatrist has definitely got his ᵇ(*neck and neck/work cut out/liberties taken/shoulder chipped*).

10. He had no intention of standing for Parliament, but he was ᵃ(*bowled over by/roped into/fobbed off/easily led by*) the election at the last moment, and now he and his rival candidate are ᵇ(*neck and neck/petty/on their high horses/out of the woods*). I wouldn't like to predict the outcome.

11. As we were all ᵃ(*set in our ways/about to reek/on tenterhooks/batting an eyelid*) waiting for your exam results, I ᵇ(*rang a bell/bailed out/pulled my weight/took the liberty*) of opening an official letter addressed to you. Perhaps it wasn't a very ᶜ(*petty/shrewd/uplifting/godsending*) move. You failed!

12. *Even at the age of 45, my childish husband still goes through* ª(fads/field days/binges/ liberties) *in his musical preferences. I'm quite the opposite; I don't like change in anything. I have become quite* ᵇ(a plodder/shrewd/set in my ways/bowled over) *in my old age.*

13. *After three hours of walking in the stifling heat, we all began to* ª(binge/rope in/have a field day/reek) *of sweat. Not very pleasant, I know. But we* ᵇ(fobbed off/plodded on/pulled our weight/rang a bell) *without a care in the world.*

14. *I can completely understand why the German public are not exactly* ª(bowled over/taking liberties/flogging a dead horse/pulling their weight) *by the idea of their government having to* ᵇ(steal the thunder of/bail out/fob off/live up to) *other less well-off European countries.*

Lesson One

To ring-fence (To prohibit money intended for a specific purpose being spent on another purpose)

Examples:
- Treasury Minister:
  *Just because we have **ring-fenced** education and health against cuts, it doesn't mean we cannot strive to make efficiency savings within those departments.*
- *Parents are dismayed that the Headmaster has **ring-fenced** £500,000 for a new science block rather than investing it in the employment of better teachers. Surely, this is more crucial to the success of the school if it wants to maintain its place at the cutting edge of independent education.*

To rise to the bait (To get angry with someone who is teasing and provoking you with the sole purpose of getting you annoyed)

Examples:
- *I'm not going to **rise to the bait**, so there's no point in resorting to nasty comments. Your unpleasant, silly behaviour will be your downfall. Mark my words.*
- *Perhaps I shouldn't have told him that if he were to step down as managing director, nobody would mourn his loss. Fortunately, he didn't **rise to the bait**.*

"I don't/can't blame you!" ("I understand why you think that way/did that thing")

Examples:
- A: *I'm fed up with Peter taking liberties with me. I know everyone thinks I have a big chip on my shoulder, but I've had enough and I'm leaving him.*
  B: ***I don't blame you!***
- ***You can't blame us*** *for firing him. He hardly ever met deadlines and had a spate of affairs with some of our female clients.*

To take the biscuit (To be the worst or most extreme example)--*a light-hearted negative expression,*)

Examples:
- *When it comes to whingeing, Tom **takes the biscuit**. He's even worse than your mother, who is also somewhat prone to making an unnecessary fuss.*
- A: *Asking her father for specific advice about the business might have sparked debate amongst her partners, but inviting him to meetings really does **take the biscuit**, don't you think?*
- B: *Well, you can't blame her really. Who else can she turn to?*

To boycott, a boycott (To stop trading/having relations with a particular company, shop or country; an agreement not to trade/have relations with a company/shop/country etc.--*usually as a punishment or way of making a protest,*)

Examples:
- *In my youth, I was proud to have convinced my parents to **boycott** South African goods during its regime of apartheid, but now in my old age, I have mellowed and can't be bothered with half the world's problems.*
- *I'm not sure that there is such a gulf, as is claimed, between those governments that believe in military intervention against Iran and others that would prefer to implement a trade **boycott**. Neither will lead to a satisfactory conclusion.*

Role reversal (A situation where jobs or expected behaviour are swapped/reversed)

Examples:
- *I've lost track of how many times I've had to correct my son's teacher on his poor grammar and non-existent punctuation, and he's always giving me handy tips on how to stop him bickering with his sister. It's a complete **role reversal** between teacher and parent.*
- *It's clear that Patricia, the younger one of the two sisters, acts a lot more responsibly and is evidently more reliable when the family have problems to sort out. Her elder sister Gillian, however, is much more immature and can be vindictive towards Patricia. Gillian clearly struggles with this **role reversal**, which has unfortunately taken its toll on their relationship.*

60

Done and dusted (Finished, completed--*describing a situation where action has been taken and a problem has been resolved or a deal made*)

Examples:

- A: *That was a gruelling meeting which I wasn't looking forward to at all, but I'm glad we took the bull by the horns and got to the bottom of the problem.*

  B: *Yes, and it does feel great that it's all **done and dusted** and out of the way.*

- *The deal is **done and dusted** at last. I'm so happy about that. It seemed we were just plodding on, getting nowhere.*

*"I've lost track of how many times I've had to correct my son's teacher on his poor grammar and non-existent punctuation, and he's always giving me handy tips on how to stop him bickering with his sister. It's a complete **role reversal** between teacher and parent."* (see page 60)

An ordeal (A difficult experience, a hard time)

Examples:

- It has, to say the least, been a bit of an **ordeal**. I'm trying to banish these unpleasant memories to the back of my mind. But I no longer want to be in the limelight; I'm moving to Scotland.
- A: I wouldn't like to go through that **ordeal** again; it left me seething.

  B: Well, you'd better brace yourself: I've booked you in with the same counsellor next week.

To sneer at (To look at/speak to someone in a superior manner; to show that one considers an idea below one's social standing/capabilities)

Examples:

- When I suggested to my husband that we practise some role reversal with him doing the housework and me watching the television all evening, he simply **sneered at** me. Why should he lift a finger?
- My mother and I rallied around my grandmother when she became ill and incapacitated, but my sister, on the other hand, **sneered at** the very idea of having to wash our grandmother's clothes and clean her house. She's not renowned for being all that nice, my sister.

Much of a muchness (Not really different; more or less the same--*often negative*)

Examples:

- I can't really decide which of these guys will make a better mayor. They're **much of a muchness** to me. They both come out with ridiculous promises to change things. I think I'll go with the flow and see which one has the nicer smile on Election Day.
- A: She's not my cup of tea. I prefer the doctor we had before, don't you?

  B: Don't ask me; they're all **much of a muchness**. They take liberties where they can and try to fob you off with cheap medication.

Lesson Two

Gloomy, gloom (Dark and depressing; a state of darkness and depression--*often referring to the future*)

Examples:
- It was all looking **gloomy** for the economy at the time of the Government bailouts, but now the banks are making a killing once again; quite a feat when you think how many of the smaller ones were left in tatters by the credit crunch.
- The bad winter this year wreaked havoc on the livelihoods of many local farmers, but it's not all doom and **gloom**. Those who are not so set in their ways have opened their minds to attracting other means of income through tourism and selling their products online.

To sit through (To stay until the end of something very boring or of poor quality)

Examples:
- I don't blame our daughter Sofia for opting out of violin lessons next year and for us it will be heaven. But commiserations: <u>you</u> have another three years of school concerts to **sit through**.
- A: I dread the thought of **sitting through** more dinner parties with them, having to listen to their bickering.
- B: It is rather a daunting prospect, isn't it? Just turn a blind eye to it.

Excruciating (Extremely painful--*sometimes used figuratively when something is painfully bad or embarrassing*)

Examples:
- I hope you never have to go through the very unpleasant ordeal of kidney stones. The pain is **excruciating**.
- His first play was dreadful, but his latest one really takes the biscuit. Having to sit through it in the theatre for three hours was **excruciating**.

Corny (Unoriginal and unsophisticated; too sentimental)

Examples:
- I think Johnson was lured into the world of comedy writing by the prospect of fame and fortune. But his scripts are **corny**, full of clichés and in stark contrast to his earlier stunning historical dramas.

- *Every year on our wedding anniversary my husband is prone to making **corny** and fake declarations of love, but I don't bat an eyelid. I know he's just trying to make up for a year of not pulling his weight around the house.*

To close ranks (To support colleagues/partners when they come under attack, even if they are in the wrong--*often used negatively as a way of criticising such support*)

Examples:
- *If you are thinking of complaining about the Finance Director to the other members of the Board, you should be aware that you will have your work cut out. They will simply **close ranks** and stifle any form of criticism.*
- *When anyone queries why the NHS budget has not been ring-fenced, Government ministers **close ranks**. It's all a big cover-up of the blunders the Conservative Party made in promising the impossible to the voting public before they came into power.*

A: *"I dread the thought of **sitting through** more dinner parties with them, having to listen to their bickering.*
B: *It is rather a daunting prospect, isn't it? Just turn a blind eye to it."*

(see page 63)

To humour (To be nice to someone and pretend to take them seriously in order to please them or keep them content; to say "yes" just for peace and quiet)

Examples:
- A: I know you think I'm being petty with half the things I complain about, but I don't think you take in a word I say. You just **humour** me.
  B: Yes, dear.
- **Humouring** him with flattering comments about the quality of his work may have clinched the deal. Done and dusted!

To come to one's senses (To become rational after a period of doubt and uncertainty)

Examples:
- They tried to rope my son into joining their gang because they know how vulnerable and easily led he is. At first my husband and I were worried, but fortunately he has **come to his senses** and rejected them.
- He has been lured away from the city by a beautiful woman renowned for her temper tantrums. I don't know what to do to make him **come to his senses**.

To have a/the knack for (To have a special skill for doing something-- *sometimes used humorously/sarcastically to describe a skill for doing something wrong—see 2nd example below*)

Examples:
- Pete's sudden appearance with a bag of tools was a godsend. I don't really **have the knack for** fixing things and DIY (do-it-yourself).
- She's not vindictive; she just has a **real knack for** not thinking about what she's saying. But you can't blame people for getting upset.

The penny has dropped (A situation or concept has been understood only after a long period of not understanding)

Examples:
- For the last month she has had many strange cravings during the night, but **the penny** doesn't seem to have **dropped** with her husband that she is pregnant. Maybe he has banished the idea of his wife ever getting pregnant again after a spate of miscarriages.

- *The reason why he's looking so glum is that **the penny** has finally **dropped**. He was wrong to stick to his guns; continuing the business in the current economic climate is like flogging a dead horse.*

Detractor (A person who doesn't like someone or their work/beliefs--*generally used in the plural*)

Examples:
- *She had a few **detractors** who tried to organise a boycott of her concerts, but her friends and genuine fans closed ranks and the show went ahead unhampered.*
- *Even though his **detractors** will claim he was a hardliner, he never resorted to underhand tactics to get what he wanted.*

Lesson Three

To rekindle (To relight or revive--*usually refers to one's passion for something or someone*)

Examples:
- *I was right to be a little bit wary of taking up a new sport at my age. I clearly didn't have the knack for golf. Instead, I decided to **rekindle** my passion for tennis, which I played as a youngster.*
- *Since my youngest son left home to go to university, my husband and I have found time to **rekindle** our love for each other. I know it sounds corny, but it has been an uplifting experience for us both.*

To ruffle someone's feathers (To annoy/upset)

Examples:
- *His feathers were definitely **ruffled** when you stole his thunder. Mind you, there was no need for him to get on his high horse about it.*
- *You clearly **ruffled** the Headmaster's feathers by bringing up the palaver of last year's exams. Let's hope he steps down soon before he loses his marbles completely.*

Red tape (Bureaucracy)

Examples:
- *These two schemes the Government are considering implementing are much of a muchness. Neither will cut through the **red tape** which has hampered the smooth running of the recruitment industry in recent years. The whole system needs overhauling.*
- *At last the penny seems to have dropped: the Mayor now realises his detractors have a point. There's too much **red tape** in local government administration.*

To read between the lines (To understand that there are meanings which don't appear on the surface/are not explicitly stated)

Examples:
- ***Reading between the lines**, he doesn't seem to relish the idea of rekindling their relationship. Perhaps letting her move back in with him was not the shrewdest of decisions.*

- *Their true intention with the release of this statement is to fob us off. **Read between the lines** and you'll see what I mean. But we must stick to our guns.*

Uncanny (Unusual and inexplicable, mysterious--*generally used to describe a situation, often a coincidence, or someone's ability, rather than an individual person. One would not say, for example, "He is uncanny.")*

Examples:
- A: *It's **uncanny** how every person we've taken on in summer interviews has not lived up to our expectations.*

  B: *We'll have our work cut out in July, then.*
- *He has the **uncanny** knack of clinching victory with a goal in the dying seconds of the game.*

To pass the buck (To refuse to take any responsibility when things go wrong and to blame others for it--*note the expression **"the buck stops with me"** which means "I accept that I, and no one else, must take responsibility for anything that goes wrong")*

Examples:
- *The England manager **passed the buck**, blaming many of his players for not pulling their weight. His unwillingness to take responsibility does not bode well for the future of the team, but the Football Association don't want to ruffle his feathers.*
- *I'd just like to chip in by saying that all the directors on the board understand that the **buck stops with us**. If we're not out of the woods by this time next year, our jobs will be on the line.*

To do away with (To get rid of)

Examples:
- *Every in-coming politician, local or national, promises **to do away with** red tape until it dawns on them that <u>they</u> are the red tape.*
- *Many parents at the school sneered at the Headmaster's idea of **doing away with** spelling correction. He said it might wreak havoc with the pupils 'confidence as they progress into adulthood. Reading between the lines, I think what he really means is that he wants to reduce the workload for his staff. I despair!*

Rule of thumb (A principle based on experience rather than theory)

Examples:
- There is one **rule of thumb** I always stick to: I never rekindle old relationships.
- Whatever problems come my mum's way, she will always plod on regardless. Being positive and cheerful at all times is a **rule of thumb** which has stood her in good stead over the years.

To spur on (To encourage, to inspire; to make someone/a group of people try harder)

Examples:
- Even though we were clearly the underdogs, our supporters **spurred us on** to victory.
- I have always strived for excellence in everything I do because I was constantly **spurred on** by my parents, who believed in me. This was in stark contrast to the way they were brought up themselves.
  (see picture below)

To peak   (To achieve a maximum of development/standard/readiness at a specific period of time)

Examples:
- We're all on tenterhooks to see how he did in his exams. I do hope he didn't **peak** too early in his preparation and revision.
- As a young tennis star she **peaked** at fourteen. After that, I'm afraid, relentless coaching and physical conditioning stifled her progress in professional competitions. Great pity.

Chapter Five in Use
Listen to the CD - Track 6

TWO MOTHERS HAVING A CHAT OUTSIDE THEIR CHILDREN'S SCHOOL

HELEN: *Hello Alison, how are you? Haven't seen you for ages.*

ALISON: *I'm fine, thanks. I've been very busy looking at secondary schools for my eldest, Joshua. It's been quite an* ordeal, *I can tell you*

HELEN: *Which one did you go for?*

ALISON: *Well, they're all* much of a muchness *in the end. We've had to* sit through *so many parents' evenings listening to boring head teacher speeches.*

HELEN: *…with their* corny *jokes?*

ALISON: *Absolutely! I can see you've been through the same thing.*

HELEN: *Oh yes, an* excruciating *experience, and one which I don't relish having to go through again for my youngest, Katherine.*

ALISON: *Anyway, in the end we opted for the local boys' Catholic school, St. Dominic's. It has an excellent academic record and the boys are taught discipline. But I've been amazed at how many parents at Josh's current school – mothers actually, more than fathers – have* sneered at *my husband and me because of our decision. One mother even told me that she thought religious schools should be* done away with.

HELEN: *I can imagine who that was. Well,* I don't blame you *at all. One* rule of thumb *I stick to is that I don't comment on what other people decide for their children.*

ALISON: *Mind you, I have to say there's a lot of* red tape *you have to cut through to get into religious schools. And some of the questions you have to answer, like "How many times do you pray a day?" That really* takes the biscuit. *Anyway, it's all* done and dusted *now. St. Dominic's is where he's going…And what have you been up to? Sorry, it's all been about me.*

HELEN: *Oh don't worry, I understand. We've been fine, actually. Gerry has* rekindled *his love for tennis…he* has a knack for *racket sports. And I've taken up writing short stories while Gerry cooks for the kids…a bit of* role reversal *there. My sister is a professional writer and her success has* spurred me on *to have a go at it myself.*

ALISON: *And has she read any of your stuff?*

HELEN: *Bits and pieces…but I prefer her not to; she tends to* humour *me, and more to the point has an* uncanny *habit of subtly telling me where my writing is just not good enough. This really gets* to me and I'm afraid I often *rise to the bait*.

ALISON: *Oh, here come our kids, laughing together. How nice! Let's continue this chat tomorrow. I'm fascinated to hear more about your writing.*

HELEN: *Liar!*

ALISON: *Ha ha! OK …see you tomorrow.*

The outlook for the British economy

I have to start off by saying that it's very difficult not to be gloomy *when it comes to both the short and long terms for the economy in the UK.*

The Chancellor, Francis Hopkins, who in the UK is ultimately responsible for all financial aspects of Government, has his detractors, *and, to be honest, it can be very hard to* read between the lines *when assessing his statements. What is he really trying to tell us? He seems very ready to* pass the buck *and blame everybody else apart from his own Government for creating such a large deficit. And yet he has* ring-fenced *the budgets of certain departments from cutbacks to expenditure – departments which have wasted huge amounts of money for many years. Does he realise this? Has the* penny dropped? *One wonders.*

It is time for him and the Prime Minister to come to their senses. *It's no good simply* closing ranks *when Government policy is criticised or when a cabinet minister's* feathers *have been* ruffled.

Not only do we need to see a clear, well-structured approach to dealing with the deficit, but also optimistic and inspiring policies to promote economic growth in all parts of the country. Why, for example, have so many multinational companies boycotted *northern regions of England, where rents are cheap and corporation tax low? Business, especially international business, is so focused on London, a great business-friendly city, I agree…but one which has surely* peaked.

I told you I was going to be gloomy.

72

Chapter Five: **Exercise**

CHOOSE THE CORRECT WORD FROM THOSE IN GREEN
Answers on page 139

1. A: One ᵃ(detractor/rule of thumb/ordeal/boycott) I try to stick to is that if someone consistently ᵇ(comes to their senses/drops the penny/reads between the lines/ruffles my feathers), I cut them out of my life. I don't want anything to do with them.
   B: That's a bit over the top, don't you think? You must admit, you do tend to ᶜ(rise to the bait/sneer/pass the buck/take the biscuit) a bit too easily.

2. A: It was absolutely ᵃ(excruciating/gloomy/corny/done and dusted) having to listen to her 10-year-old son "play" the violin.
   B: Oh yes…and it was even more ᵇ(a boycott/a detractor/of an ordeal/uncanny) watching her daughter in the school play.
   A: When she asks us what we thought of their performances, we will just have to ᶜ(rekindle/humour/ruffle/sneer) her and say how wonderfully talented both her children are.

3. The Prime Minister has said that there will be no cuts to the defence budget. This money has been ᵃ(humoured/boycotted/ring-fenced/done away with). But ᵇ(reading between the lines/reversing the roles/taking the biscuit/closing ranks), some members of his cabinet regret this decision. It is clear to see that even at this early stage in his premiership, he has his ᶜ(ordeals/red tape/rule of thumb/detractors).

4. I've always known that John has a ᵃ(rule of thumb/knack/peak/ring-fence) for saying the wrong thing at the wrong time, but telling the boss that he didn't like his ᵇ(corny/uncanny/gloomy/rekindling) jokes was really ᶜ(reading between the lines/coming to his senses/taking the biscuit/dropping the penny).

5. I dread having to ᵃ(rise to the bait/spur on/sit through/boycott) another board meeting, when everyone knows all the directors are going to ᵇ(ruffle their feathers/pass the buck/ring-fence/rise to the bait) and blame the state of the economy for the company's misfortunes. I ask myself, "When are they going to ᶜ(come to their senses/read between the lines/take the biscuit/reverse the roles) and take some responsibility?"

6. A: In her retirement, my mum has ᵃ(peaked/rekindled/humoured/sneered at) her passion for gardening. She was ᵇ(done and dusted/boycotted/spurred on/ring-fenced) by my dad, who has offered to take over kitchen and housework duties.
   B: How interesting! A bit of ᶜ(passing the buck/red tape/closing ranks/role reversal) there?

7. A: I've decided to ᵃ(boycott/ring-fence/sit through/spur on) my local so-called independent baker, who keeps whingeing about people using supermarkets instead of individual shops. He wants to charge me £4 for a loaf of bread. I'm not paying it.
B: I ᵇ(would reverse the roles/ruffle his feathers/have a knack/don't blame you). I have told my butcher the very same thing many times, but I don't think ᶜ(it's an ordeal/the penny has dropped/it's done and dusted/he has passed the buck).

8. It's ᵃ(gloomy/much of a muchness/uncanny/corny) how every time I think there may be a chance that at least one of my bosses is taking my side, they all ᵇ(close ranks/sneer/rise to the bait/read between the lines) and ᶜ(rekindle/sneer at/sit through/do away with) me.

9. A: I still can't decide who to vote for. All the parties are ᵃ(an ordeal/done and dusted/much of a muchness/taking the biscuit).
B: I totally agree. If I had my way, I would ᵇ(pass the buck/humour/sneer at/ do away with) all of them. I could sort out all of the country's problems in ten minutes. There we are, all ᶜ(done and dusted/boycotted/much of a muchness/the penny has dropped)!

10. A: I tell you what: cutting the ᵃ(ordeal/red tape/detractors/boycotts) which local businesses have to comply with these days will contribute greatly to lifting the current ᵇ(rule of thumb/ordeal/gloom/bait) surrounding local enterprise.
B: Oh, it would indeed. And it's such a shame to see good businesses struggling to survive through no fault of their own. Many of them should be ᶜ(sneering/peaking/spurring on/rising to the bait) at this time of year, just before Christmas.

Lesson One

Red herring (A clue/piece of information which initially looks important, but is in fact irrelevant and distracts attention from the real issue)

> Examples:
> * The police superintendent simply passed the buck when he was accused of following too many **red herrings** in this murder investigation. I know this for sure because I heard it from the horse's mouth: Peter.
> * For your exams it is absolutely crucial that you mug up on your subjects thoroughly and then read the questions carefully on the day. Be particularly wary of **red herrings**, which are designed to lead you in the wrong direction.

To clash

> **i.** (To get on badly/disagree with someone)
> Examples:
> * Even though my brother and I have mellowed as the years have gone by, we still sometimes **clash** <u>on</u> many issues and have both become very set in our ways.
> * The Prime Minister and the Leader of the Opposition have **clashed** <u>over</u> the ring-fencing of Defence spending. It has been suggested that the production of military helicopters needs to be stepped up.

> **ii.** (Not to match in colour)
> Examples:
> * A: This style of wallpaper is just a fad and in this room it will **clash** with the carpet. A rule of thumb which I will advise my daughter to adhere to is never trust men when it comes to colour schemes.
> * B: Oh women! Why are you all so petty?

Stickler (A person with attention to tiny detail/who cannot tolerate mistakes--*used in a specific rather than general sense, focusing on one subject. It is often followed by "for"*)

> Examples:
> * I'm a bit of a **stickler** <u>for</u> good, grammatical English and yours is deplorable. I mourn the days when grammar was taught in our schools.

- *The boss is a real **stickler** <u>for</u> meeting deadlines, so don't try to pass the buck. All hell breaks loose in this office when things don't go to plan; you'll see.*

Disarray (A state of confusion and disorder)

Examples:
- *The outlook for the economy in the UK will continue to be gloomy whilst the welfare benefits system is <u>in</u> **disarray**.*
- *My father always sneered at my mother's attempts to spur me on to greater things. Little did I know at the time that his own life was <u>in</u> such **disarray**.*

A: *"This style of wallpaper is just a fad and in this room it will **clash** with the carpet. A rule of thumb which I will advise my daughter to adhere to is never trust men when it comes to colour schemes.*
B: *Oh women! Why are you all so petty?"*

(see page 75)

To feel the pinch (To have money problems)

Examples:
- Reading between the lines, I think he is **feeling the pinch**. He has had to resort to asking his parents-in-law to pay the kids' school fees.
- When the economic crisis first hit this country, our livelihoods were not really affected, but as it has gathered momentum, we have begun to **feel the pinch**.

To be vindicated (To be proved right, to be justified in having a controversial opinion--*note that the vindication usually occurs at a later stage rather than immediately*)

Examples:
- Our fears that the council's new housing plans were in complete disarray have **been vindicated**…and from now on I'm boycotting any of their excruciatingly boring meetings.
- He has been criticised for being too much of a hardliner and a bit of a stickler as far as punctuality is concerned. But I'm sure most of the ruthless decisions he has made will **be vindicated** in the not too distant future.

A blow (An emotional shock--*often caused by bad news--note also the expression "**to soften/cushion the blow**", which means to make bad news a little less unpleasant*)

Examples:
- It came as a real **blow** to hear about your dad's passing away, but at least he had his whole family rallying around him during his final days.
- It was a bit of a **blow** to his self-esteem when his film didn't go down well with any of the celebrated film critics. His feathers have clearly been ruffled.
- In order to **soften/cushion** the blow of making us work longer hours, the boss has offered to do away with the system of having to sign in and out whenever we enter or leave the building. Big deal!

To pull someone up on something (To criticise someone for small mistakes--*see for the same meaning "**to pick someone up on something**", Practical Everyday English, page 75, meaning ix*)

Examples:
- My mother-in-law **pulls me up on** everything I do - and don't do - with the children. She's a stickler for strict discipline and definitely lives up to the scary mother-in-law image.

- *I don't want to keep **pulling you up on** what might seem to you to be petty errors, but I think you're chasing red herrings. I feel I must step in when my instructions are not being implemented.*

The jury is still out (It's too early to form an opinion)

Examples:
- *He is poised to make his first England appearance and many football journalists believe he is peaking at the right time, **but the jury is still out**. Let's wait and see how he gets on before we pass judgement.*
- A: *Nobody can quite understand why she agreed to take on the burden of running a failing school. A school which the whole country seems to know about.*

  B: *Maybe she just likes being in the limelight. Who knows? Anyway, she seems to have made a decent start...although **the jury is still out**. I've seen a lot of head teachers come and go.*

Insight, insightful (A deep understanding of an issue; deeply observant)

Examples:
- *It was a severe blow to discover that the accounts of the company were in total disarray, but it has given me an **insight** <u>into</u> how not to run a business.*
- *Her comments about how we might consider launching new products and that persisting with the old ones was flogging a dead horse were most **insightful**.*

Lesson Two

An accident waiting to happen (An accident/tragedy which is likely to happen because appropriate precautions are not being taken)

Examples:
- *The hospital management team had neglected to implement any of the Health Authority's suggestions to improve patient care, particularly of the elderly. This poor old lady's unnecessary death, caused by the blunders of medical staff, was **an accident waiting to happen**.*
- *Since the last tenants were evicted, the property has fallen into a state of disrepair. The landlord has overlooked many safety issues which need addressing. It's **an accident waiting to happen**. (see picture below)*

To put on a brave face   (To act as if one is coping with a situation or life in general, but is in fact struggling--*note one can also say "to put a brave face <u>on it</u>". See 2nd example below*)

Examples:

- *In the wake of her son's disappearance, she has somehow managed to **put on a brave face**, but in truth her life is in tatters.*
- *I feel very vulnerable at the moment, and my energy levels are depleted, but I still find the strength to **put a brave face** on it. I don't want to come over as being too gloomy.*

To be in the same boat   (To be in the same bad situation as someone else)

Examples:

- *We're all **in the same boat**. The situation is farcical. We're doomed!*
- *It's comforting to know that however much this unpleasant experience has taken its toll on our lives, we are **in the same boat** and will come through it together.*

To unveil   (To present to the public--*an object or plans, not a person*)

Examples:

- *A new statue of Charles Dickens was **unveiled** in the town centre last week to commemorate 200 years since his birth. Some idiot shouted, "It's a fake!" A fake of what, exactly? Nobody has claimed it to be an old masterpiece sculpture, so what was he talking about?*
- *Minister, when is the Government going to **unveil** its plans to outlaw binge drinking in our towns and cities?*

Upheaval   (A very big and inconvenient change)

Examples:

- *You may be able to put on a brave face at the thought of our move abroad, but for me it's a massive **upheaval** that I could do without.*
- *What an **upheaval** changing hotels in the middle of a holiday can be. The one where we were staying reeked of cigarette smoke, and the staff were in total disarray when we all arrived. The name of the one we are at now rang a bell, so we thought we might as well give it a go. I do hope it's worth the hassle.*

Shortcomings (Faults, defects)

Examples:
- *He may well be a shrewd and talented politician, but as a husband, he has many **shortcomings**.*
- *One rule of thumb: don't list his **shortcomings** in front of his detractors. That would be unprofessional.*

To play it by ear (To see how things go before making any decisions)

Examples:
- *We have been vindicated by our research, which has given us a true insight into what is going on at Head Office…but I still think we should **play it by ear**.*
- A: *I can't decide which of these two courses to go for; they're much of a muchness.*
- B: *We're in exactly the same boat, but let's just **play it by ear**; we've got time on our side.*

In the nick of time (Just in time)

Examples:
- *We got there **in the nick of time**, but then had to sit through a very boring introductory lecture…and later I got roped into joining the entertainment committee. So, quite an ordeal in the end.*
- *As it turned out, I got the job done just **in the nick of time**, but I had to apologise for leaving everybody on tenterhooks until the very last minute.*

To mount up (To get bigger/more numerous--*usually cost or problems*)

Examples:
- A: *Breakfast is not included (unlike in the UK), so firstly you have to go through the palaver of the whole family agreeing where to go. I'm not exactly bowled over by continental breakfasts, and once we've all had our brioches and extra strong coffees, that's goodbye to 70 euros. **It mounts up!** Next year I'm staying at home.*
- B: *I don't blame you.*
- *Charging us for books on top of ordinary school fees is really taking the biscuit. I always read these invoices with a glum look on my face. Before you know where you are, **it has mounted up**.*

- *You mustn't allow relationship problems to **mount up**. Nip them in the bud immediately. Reading between the lines of what you've been telling me over the last hour, I think you may have already realised that I am right. The penny has dropped, yes?*

To squander (To waste, to fail to take advantage of)

Examples:
- *Local councils in this part of the country have for many years taken liberties with their citizens' money. How they manage to **squander** such vast sums on pointless projects never ceases to amaze me. And heads don't seem to roll.*
- *I think he peaked with the rock album he made in 2003. Since then, he has **squandered** his musical talent and produces bland rubbish for teenagers and their infantile parents.*

Lesson Three

Bereft (Lacking, without--*generally used with "of"*)

Examples:
- *I don't know how they managed to lose three games in a row. They squandered so many chances and seem to be **bereft** of ideas in midfield.*
- ***Bereft** of a loving family, he grew up with a big chip on his shoulder. Maria coming into his life has been a godsend.*

To beggar belief (To be unbelievable--*generally used to describe unbelievable incompetence or stupidity*)

Examples:
- *How these fat cats have been allowed to make such a killing while the rest of us are feeling the pinch **beggars belief**.*
- A: *The student loans company admit to having lost 5,000 applications even though they claim to have done away with the old computer system and implemented improvements.*
- B: *Yes, utterly useless. Their incompetence **beggars belief**, doesn't it?*

Rash/Hasty (Too quick--*used where there has been a lack of thought/consideration*)

Examples:
- *He is too shrewd to make any **rash** decisions that later he may live to regret. I'm sure his long term plans will soon be unveiled.*
- A: *Let's do away with all red tape immediately.*
- B: *Don't you think you're being a bit **hasty**? We do need some regulation in this business.*

Gall, galling (Cheek/impudence/audacity; irritating/infuriating--*used by someone who is angered by another person's rude and direct behaviour*)

Examples:
- *She, of all people, has **the gall** to call my books corny and bereft of imagination. That really takes the biscuit!*
- *I don't know how you have **the gall** to come here and tell me that my beloved son is not your cup of tea. He is renowned for his good looks and superior intelligence. Your loss!*

- *It's really **galling** to see so many fat cats getting away with murder, when for the rest of us everyday expenses are mounting up.*

To get one's just deserts (To get the punishment one deserves)

Examples:
- *My doubts about her have been completely vindicated and I'm glad to hear she has **got her just deserts**.*
- *Don't let yourself rise to the bait. I don't know how he has the gall to talk to you like that, actually. But don't worry: people like him always get **their just deserts**.*

To vilify (To abuse someone verbally, to criticise someone strongly in public--*generally used in the passive voice*)

Examples:
- *He has been **vilified** in the press for all his shortcomings, but he has managed to put a brave face on it and is getting on with his life.*
- *In the wake of the very public row they had on a television news channel last week, where they clashed over the Government's immigration policy, they have both been **vilified** by their detractors.*

To put someone in their place (To shut someone up and make them realise that they don't know what they are talking about)

Examples:
- *My English friend sneered at my attempts to speak French, saying that I sounded very English. I didn't bat an eyelid, but his French wife chipped in by telling us that her husband's French made her the laughing stock of the village. That **put him in his place**.*
- A: *This wind is wreaking havoc with my hair.*
  B: *Don't worry, it already looked stupid anyway.*
  A: *Well at least I have some hair, even if it does look stupid.*
  B: *Ooh! That's **putting me in my place**.*

Reckless (Very careless, without paying attention to danger)

Examples:
- *He has always acted **recklessly**, not considering anyone, even himself. It was an accident waiting to happen and now he has got his just deserts.*

- Even though he has been convicted on several occasions for **reckless** driving, the penny still hasn't dropped. Why he is still allowed to get behind a steering wheel beggars belief.

A: "This wind is wreaking havoc with my hair.
B: Don't worry, it already looked stupid anyway.
A: Well at least <u>I</u> have some hair, even if it does look stupid.
B: Ooh! That's **putting me in my place**."

(see page 84)

To fall from/out of grace (To become out of favour with someone of importance or the public)

Examples:
- Nobody quite knew for sure why he **fell out of grace** with Queen Victoria in her latter years. It may well be that he too often had the gall to question her judgement on family matters.

85

- A: *I think I have **fallen from grace** with my wife's parents.*
- B: *Why? What have you done?*
- A: *I put my arrogant father-in-law in his place by telling him it was an ordeal having to sit through one of his boring concerts.*
- B: *Oh dear!*

Bleary-eyed (Very tired from exhaustion or lack of sleep)

Examples:

- *I was feeling **bleary-eyed** and emotional. The last thing I needed was you patronising me in front of all my friends. Sorry to get on my high horse about it, but it's not the first time you've done it.*
- *He is looking so **bleary-eyed** and bereft of life, I only hope that he doesn't make any rash decisions.*

Chapter Six in Use

TV MORNING NEWS PROGRAMME WITH JOURNALISTS REVIEWING THE NEWSPAPERS

LYNNE: *Good morning everybody. I'm Lynne Taylor. Welcome to this morning's News Review. To look at the papers today we have Jasmine Green from The Guardian, Luke Brown from The Daily Telegraph and Greg Flanders from The Sun. Now, plenty going on this morning. Anything that catches your eye, Luke?*

LUKE: *Yes, the interview with the Leader of the Opposition, Ed Miliband, in Jasmine's paper. This Guardian piece was most insightful and surprisingly unbiased.*

JASMINE… *unlike your paper, The Telegraph. Never one-sided, of course.*

LYNNE: *Oh that put you in your place, Luke.*

LUKE: *As I was saying before being so rudely interrupted, this interview was done after he clashed with the Prime Minister in Parliament last week. He says the Government are in complete disarray over the riots, which took place all over the country last month. But he has also praised the PM for not doing anything too hasty, like suspending benefit payments of those who took part. Reading between the lines, he clearly feels he and the PM are in the same boat. Neither appears willing to unveil radical policies which will bring about real change to people's lives…but I was impressed by his measured words. He criticised the PM without vilifying him…and sort of admitted to his own party's shortcomings. They have also been bereft of ideas.*

LYNNE: *Very British honesty, one might say.*

LUKE: *Indeed.*

LYNNE: *Jasmine, what have you found for us?*

JASMINE: *A nice little story in Greg's paper.*

GREG: *Jasmine from The Guardian reading The Sun? That really does beggar belief!*

JASMINE: *Ha-ha. Well, we all have our embarrassing secrets. No, really, a lovely story. A blind man was walking along the main road of his home town with his guide dog, Bertie. Suddenly, a very old lady appeared from a side street and was about to cross the main road without looking. Bertie let out an enormous bark just in the nick of time as a reckless driver was about to run over this lady. Apparently, this crossroads has often been described as an accident waiting to happen. And that, quite literally, is what it was. Anyway, the drunk, bleary-eyed driver got his just deserts by being heavily fined for drink driving and having his licence suspended for a year. And the little old lady got to give Bertie a lovely meaty bone donated by the local butcher.*

LYNNE: *What a lovely story indeed. Now Greg, your turn. Anything in the sports pages which takes your fancy?*

GREG: *How did you guess? It's in the Independent. Rumour has it that Chelsea Football Club are feeling the pinch.*

LYNNE: *Chelsea? You're kidding?*

GREG: *The Independent doesn't joke. You should know that Lynne. The new manager, Jack Lawson, - the jury is still out over him, by the way - has been pulled up by the chairman for wanting to spend too much money. Costs are mounting up. No more money is to be squandered on past-it strikers. The fans will be delighted.*

LYNNE: *On that cheerful note, it's time for a break. See you in a few minutes.*

THOUGHTS OF A FRUSTRATED BUSINESSWOMAN

It is now November and the predictions my husband made at the beginning of the year about our business, a small chain of restaurants in North West London, have unfortunately been vindicated. He could see we were going to have problems. I was hoping, perhaps rather unrealistically, that the loss we made in January was merely a red herring and that business would pick up by the spring. I wanted to play it by ear and not do anything too rash.

But now is the time to act. Despite my general optimism, I am a stickler for detail and good planning, and I have, in my long career in the restaurant trade, seen far too many big-name places fall from grace. The owners often try to put on a brave face when business is bad, but sometimes you just have to be frank with yourself and change the way you've been running things, in spite of the upheaval this causes.

This is precisely what we need to do in our business if we want to succeed. And some people have the gall to say I'm past it. To be honest, it would be a terrible blow for me if they were proved right.

But I'm not past it, by any stretch of the imagination. As the great song says, "I will survive!"

Chapter Six: Exercise

CHOOSE THE CORRECT WORD FROM THOSE IN GREEN
Answers on page 140

1. At the moment money is tight and we are definitely ᵃ(*mounting up/feeling the pinch/getting our just deserts/bleary-eyed*), but I don't know how things are going to turn out next year, so I'll just have to ᵇ(*fall from grace/squander/play it by ear/be reckless*) and see what happens. However, last year I said we weren't going to be able to pay all our expenses, and I was ᶜ(*vindicated/clashed/reckless/mounted up*). Believe me, I wish I had been proved wrong.

2. The manager has acted ᵃ(*in disarray/recklessly/rash/insightfully*) in ᵇ(*clashing/vindicating/falling from grace/squandering*) money on footballers who are clearly not good enough for the Premiership. No wonder he has been ᶜ(*clashed/vindicated/vilified/bereft*) in the press.

3. A: We got here just ᵃ(*in the nick of time/unveiled/recklessly/bleary-eyed*). One minute later and my plans for the rest of the day would have been in ᵇ(*the nick of time/galling/disarray/upheaval*).
   B: And you look a bit ᶜ(*vindicated/feeling the pinch/bereft/bleary-eyed*) this morning, if you don't mind my saying.

4. A: Moving offices, especially at this busy time of year, has been such ᵃ(*a disarray/an upheaval/a blow/a fall from grace*). And you've no idea how quickly costs ᵇ(*squander/clash/feel the pinch/mount up*).
   B: But in the end was the move worthwhile?
   A: I don't know. Too early to say. ᶜ(*The jury is still out/The move was reckless/There are shortcomings/It was an accident waiting to happen*).

5. In this case I think the police were ᵃ(*reckless/hasty/bereft/vilified*) of real, hard evidence. The fact that the two boys were in the same class at school was clearly irrelevant. It was a ᵇ(*red herring/stickler/clash/upheaval*), which didn't warrant being followed up. Quite honestly it ᶜ(*beggars belief/is galling/is a blow/mounts up*) how this case ever got to court in the first place.

6. A: This is very bad news indeed. I don't know how I'm going to tell him. What can I say to ᵃ(*vilify him/fall from grace/pull him up/soften the blow*)?
   B: Nothing. I think he's just going to have to ᵇ(*fall from grace/put on a brave face/beggar belief/be in the same boat*) and deal with the challenge ahead.
   A: Well, let's just take it one step at a time. I don't want to act too ᶜ(*hastily/bleary-eyed/reckless/bereft*).

7. It's such a great pity, especially for my mother, that my sister and I ᵃ(*get our just deserts/beggar belief/clash/squander*) whenever we get together. I know I have my own ᵇ(*sticklers/upheaval/red herrings/shortcomings*). Nobody's perfect. But I cannot stand her ᶜ(*pulling me up/mounting up/feeling the pinch/clashing*) on everything I say. It really gets to me.

8.	A: I know he is ᵃ(a red herring/a stickler/reckless/in disarray) for getting things right, but I don't know how he had the ᵇ(upheaval/shortcomings/stickler/gall) to show me up in front of my colleagues. Unforgiveable!
	B: I hope you ᶜ(put on a brave face/put him in his place/pull him up/felt the pinch). He shouldn't be allowed to get away with that sort of behaviour.

9.	Having had the opportunity to look at the plans for the new suspension bridge before they were ᵃ(unveiled/clashed/vilified/vindicated) to the planning officers, I felt that I had been given a proper ᵇ(disarray/upheaval/insight/stickler) into how structural engineers go about their business. In this case I'm not so sure that all of them are convinced how safe the bridge will be. It could be ᶜ(an upheaval/an accident waiting to happen/a red herring/reckless).

10.	A: I suppose it's some consolation that we are ᵃ(in disarray/bereft/an accident waiting to happen/in the same boat), both apparently having ᵇ(squandered/played it by ear/shortcomings/fallen from grace) with our once adoring fans.
	B: Yes it is. I imagine that some critics will say that as neither of us has written any decent songs for many years, we have ᶜ(got our just deserts/vilified/been insightful/softened the blow).

Lesson One

To grumble (To complain--*often used with "I mustn't/shouldn't"*)

Examples:
- A: *I don't blame you for not wanting to rekindle things with James. You always clashed. Besides, you've got a lot going for you in your life now and his is in such disarray, don't you agree?*
  B: *Yes, I suppose you're right. I <u>mustn't</u>* **grumble***.*
- *She's just a busybody, always interfering and* **grumbling** *about something. She has become a real burden on our lives.*

Level-headed (Balanced, rational, sensible)

Examples:
- *Unlike his brother, who is prone to tantrums, Steve is very* **level-headed***. He has the gift of the gab too, so I'm sure you'll find his company uplifting.*
- *We need to take a* **level-headed** *approach in these negotiations and be careful not to ruffle anyone's feathers.*

To override (To go against another person's formal wishes/decision, to prevail over/ supersede/replace--*note also the adjective "***overriding***", which means more important than anything else*.)

Examples:
- *Fortunately, our decision to* **override** *the shareholders' wishes has been vindicated. Thankfully, the majority of them have remained level-headed.*
- *The new law on food labelling will* **override** *all previous legislation in this area, but it will be implemented over a period of time, not immediately*
- *The* **overriding** *purpose of our dealings with the holiday company was to secure full reimbursement for our clients.*

Knock-on effect (Secondary or further effect--*used where an action or event causes another to follow*)

Examples:
- *Teachers often claim they are vilified by parents and in the right-wing press, but what many of them don't realise is that poor teaching has **knock-on effects** for children in their future lives.*
- *Low interest rates barely affect those who have squandered their earnings over the years, but for those saving for retirement they have a **knock-on effect**, reducing their livelihoods and forcing them to plod on with uninspiring jobs.*

To take it on the chin (To face/accept criticism and negative feedback without getting upset)

Examples:
- A:	*My overriding piece of advice to you is to **take** all criticism **on the chin** and don't grumble too much.*

  B:	*That's easier said than done.*
- *David's boss pulled him up on all his shortcomings, but in fairness to David, he didn't bat an eyelid and **took it all on the chin**. His level-headed reaction to criticism is to be admired.*

Littered with (Filled with errors or unpleasant things)

Examples:
- *It came as a real blow for me to discover that my son's written work was **littered with** uncorrected spelling mistakes. If it weren't such an upheaval, we'd be changing his school next term.*
- *Seeing the streets of this town **littered with** poor, starving children spurred me on to launch this new charity.*

To duck the issue/question (To avoid giving a straight answer)

Examples:
- *Instead of taking it on the chin, as a man of his maturity and experience should have done, he has **ducked the issue** and passed the buck to his colleagues.*
- *Most politicians have a knack for **ducking** journalists' **questions** and need putting in their place for doing so.*

Demise (The disappearance/end/death of something--*often gradual*)

Examples:
- Many economists are concerned that the debt crisis in Greece will have a knock-on effect in other eurozone countries. Some have even predicted the eventual **demise** of the Euro.
- The **demise** of foreign language A-level teaching in many UK secondary schools has left the translation industry bereft of good French and German speakers.

"Seeing the streets of this town **littered with** poor, starving children spurred me on to launch this new charity."

(see page 92)

To buck the trend (To go against the trend or general statistics--*generally positive, where a business is doing well while most others are suffering*)

Examples:
- Most parts of the UK have seen the rate of job losses in the private sector gather pace, but London appears to be **bucking the trend** and is still thriving.
- Many of the famous big banks lent money recklessly and squandered vast amounts of capital, but some of the smaller, lesser-known ones **bucked the trend** and are now reaping the rewards.

Lesson Two

To mull over (To consider something over a period of time, to reflect deeply on a subject)

Examples:
- *I'll **mull over** what you have suggested during the weekend, and I promise I will not duck any issues when I come back to you on Monday.*
- *The proposed contract is littered with tiny errors and, as you know, I'm a bit of a stickler for getting things right. So, let's **mull over** it for a while.*

Flavour of the month (Favourite person at the moment--*an informal expression generally used in the negative as an understatement*)

Examples:
- *Please don't patronize me…you're <u>not</u> exactly **flavour of the month** around here. I don't know how you have the gall to show your face in this house.*
- *He is <u>not</u> **flavour of the month** with his wife. Apart from the fact that he forgot her birthday, yesterday she got home from a gruelling day at work to find he had not done anything in the house. I think he has now been banished to the garden shed.*

To undercut (To sell something at a cheaper price than one's competitors)

Examples:
- *It is crucial that we don't let our rivals **undercut** us. In our heyday we never had to worry about what our competitors were up to, but now we have to plug our products and their low prices at every opportunity.*
- *My distributors never tell me the names of their customers as it would enable me to **undercut** them and sell to their customers directly. But that would not be a very shrewd move on my part, as I would lose the trust of my only distributor.*

There's no love lost between... (A polite and understated way of saying that two people don't like each other)

Examples:

- *You can see **there's no love lost between** these two actresses and they both seem to rise to each other's bait and end up seething with anger. It's quite pathetic really.*
- ***There's no love lost between** my two sisters, unfortunately. Each of them often accuses the other of doing something underhand, and neither of them are very good at taking criticism on the chin.*

To come with strings attached (To come with obligations, even though the main effect is positive)

Examples:

- *The new, lower corporation tax set by the Government has been welcomed in the business community, although it **comes with strings attached**. Nobody can now opt to be paid in share dividends instead of a salary.*
- *My dad often says: "There's no such thing as a free lunch." In other words, everything apparently good **comes with strings attached**. So, don't get too carried away with excitement, but brace yourself for a negative side to this offer.*

Par for the course (Exactly what one would expect; "Typical"--*generally used in a negative, but not very serious, sense. Note also the expression "**below par**", which means not as good as usual*).

Examples:

- A: *My brother arrived at my sister's wedding just in the nick of time, bleary-eyed from a binge-drinking session the previous night.*

  B: ***Par for the course**, really. I don't imagine he's flavour of the month with your sister?*
- *The incoming Government, which has promised to cut spending by 40%, has discovered that its own costs have mounted up to such an extent that very little in the way of savings will be made. **Par for the course**, I suppose.*
- A: *Your performance on the tennis court this afternoon is a bit **below par**, if you don't mind my saying.*

  B: *Yes, I know. I think I peaked back in the summer and it has all been going downhill since then. Mind you, I was hoping you would spur me on.*

Groggy (Tired and unsteady, finding it difficult to wake up)

Examples:
- A: I'm so **groggy** this morning, but I'd better put on a brave face and get to work.

  B: Oh stop grumbling!
- Wish me luck. I've been called in to see the boss this afternoon. I'm feeling particularly **groggy** today and not in the mood for his sneering manner.

To flick/flip through, a flick/flip through (To turn the pages of a book, brochure, magazine, etc., quite quickly; a quick turn of the pages--note also the expression "**the flip side**", which means the other side or aspect of something)

Examples:
- **Flicking through** the newspapers this morning, I got the sense that the Venezuelan president was very much put in his place by the King of Spain, who told him to shut up. Viva España !
- I had a **flick through** these two brochures. They seem much of a muchness to me. Both very colourful, but neither gave me a true insight into how these two companies operate.
- A: The **flip side** to going our separate ways is to accept that there is no love lost between us and carry on as if nothing has happened.

  B: So not facing up to reality is the answer, is it? That sounds like par for the course.

To be way off the mark (To be completely wrong)

Examples:
- I will need to mull over your proposed solution to this problem, but I have to say that your comments about how the previous administration handled the issue were **way off the mark**.
- You're **way off the mark** if you think my husband has made a killing out of the downturn in the market. The credit crunch has taken its toll on our family as much as it has yours, I can assure you.

To bear the brunt of (To come off the worst, to be hurt/damaged more than anything/anyone else)

Examples:

- Public sector workers will **bear the brunt of** the country's economic downfall. But their friends in the private sector will not be able to sneer at them, as any benefits they receive will come with strings attached.
- They were neck and neck in the race until the final bend, when our driver, Dave, was poised to win. But then, quite unwittingly, they crashed into each other, with Dave's car **bearing the brunt of** the accident. He himself, fortunately, got away with just a few cuts and bruises.

(see picture below)

Lesson Three

To enshrined in law (To transform a principle or right into law so that it is permanently protected)

Examples:
- *Many doctors believe that the right of terminally ill patients to choose to die should be **enshrined in law**. Politicians have long ducked the issue.*
- *The legal principle that a person is innocent until proven guilty is **enshrined in our law**. However, some say that this has led to many blunders committed by poorly prepared prosecution lawyers.*

To loom (To appear in the distance and threaten something unpleasant--*note also the expression "**to loom large**", which means to feature, play a major part in*)

Examples:
- *As you are all well aware, the weather has been dreadful over the last few days, with a spate of storms ruining the bank holiday weekend. And today, despite spells of patchy sunshine, clouds are **looming** overhead, and the outlook for the week is gloomy. Sorry to depress everyone.*
- *War and starvation have **loomed large** in the lives of many of these poor people. They are deeply wary of their leaders, who have squandered most of the financial aid they have received from the West.*

To strike a chord (To be of great significance to someone, to cause strong feelings of agreement in someone--*generally something which has been said*)

Examples:
- *What you said the other day about bad people never getting their just deserts really **struck a chord** with me. You're so right!*
- *The priest was hoping to **strike a chord** with the nation when he reminded us that the right to practise one's religion was enshrined in law.*

To set/get the ball rolling (To get something started)

Examples:
- We've been mulling it over for too long now. It's time to **set the ball rolling**.
- The sooner we **get the ball rolling**, the better. This deal should be done and dusted by Christmas. I hope the business will be out of the woods by then.

Whitewash (An official hiding of the truth--*note the truth in question is often unpleasant or incriminating*)

Examples:
- Many commentators believe that the enquiry into the legality of the Iraq war was a **whitewash**, and that the former Prime Minister should bear the brunt of public outrage. A few, on the other hand, feel that this is way off the mark.
- It's a complete **whitewash**. Everyone knows it. Reading between the lines, even the minister himself realises that he was lucky to get away with it. It really does beggar belief how politicians can escape justice in this country.

In a huff (In a very bad mood)

Examples:
- After the presenter had the gall to make some very unpleasant comments about her guest's fall from grace with the public, he left the studio **in a huff**. Those comments, by the way, were way off the mark.
- There was never much love lost between them, and instead of taking his unkind remarks on the chin, she went off **in a huff**.

To tick all the right boxes (To meet all the standards that are required-- *note also the expression "**box-ticking**", which describes a situation where unsatisfactory forms or reports are completed to confirm to people in authority that things are being done correctly, when in reality they may not be. It is a negative expression which suggests a more thorough system needs to be implemented*)

Examples:
- I can't say that he's <u>my</u> cup of tea, but for my sister he clearly **ticks all the right boxes**. Rather her than me!

- *The new Headmistress of my daughter's school **ticks all the right boxes**. She's done away with many outdated rules and regulations and has assured us that the buck stops with her. In addition, her promise not to raise school fees has struck a chord with parents, particularly those who are feeling the pinch.*
- *Flicking through this report, I could see straightaway that it was a whitewash. It's just **box-ticking**. Where's the detail?*

Vicious circle (A never-ending bad situation where each action taken leads to another problem, making things worse)

Examples:
- *In the wake of the world economic crash, there has been a backlash against the banks for not getting the ball rolling again by lending to small businesses. But it was their irresponsible lending which caused the crisis in the first place. It is a **vicious circle** and there appears to be no simple solution.*
- *Her life seems to be littered with health problems which she needs a level head to sort out. She has got herself trapped in a **vicious circle** of gruelling medical tests, which may not get to the bottom of her illness. In fact, they are likely to cause her even more stress, which she could really do without at the moment.*

*"I can't say that he's my cup of tea, but for my sister he clearly **ticks all the right boxes**. Rather her than me!"*

(see page 99)

To rein in (To stop/restrict/limit the actions of a powerful person or organisation-- note also "*to give free rein to*", which means to give someone complete freedom to do as they wish, often used to criticise the giving of such freedom)

Examples:

• The first thing Mrs Thatcher did when she became Prime Minister was to **rein in** the trade unions. She curbed their power to organise strikes, by enshrining in law the principle of the secret ballot; voting in private.

• I think our 18-year-old son needs to be **reined in**. He has to understand that adulthood comes with strings attached. I know it would be bucking the current trend of parents treating their children as friends, but I couldn't care less what other people do.

• The underdogs in this match were surprisingly **given free rein** to dominate the midfield, but lived up to their poor reputation in defence. The captain was particularly below par. They were consequently undone by a stupid goal they should never have given away. That's football for you.

The bottom line (The most important thing in the end, when it comes down to it--see *Practical Everyday English*, page 49, note to "when it comes to")

Examples:

• A: However much we mull over her application for the job, **the bottom line** is that she doesn't tick all the right boxes.

  B: You mean she's thick.

• My mates at work are going to have a field day when they find out what a mess I've made of organising this "bonding" weekend away for all of us. **The bottom line** is that I should never have allowed myself to get roped into doing something I know I'm not good at.

EXCHANGE OF INFORMAL EMAILS BETWEEN CLIENT AND WEB DESIGNER

Hi Jake!

How are things with you? It's been a long time.

Unfortunately, my business has really borne the brunt of the economic downturn. People just aren't spending money on household furniture and decorating these days. This has clearly had a knock-on-effect on what I sell from my website: tools and DIY equipment. I suppose I shouldn't really grumble; I've been undercutting the big DIY firms for many years and am still doing better than many of them.

Anyway, I've been mulling over some ideas on how we (or rather, you) can improve/update the website and attract more customers.
How are you fixed for time these days?

I'd like to get the ball rolling as soon as possible.
All the best

George
___

Hello George

Great to hear from you.

Yes, what you say about the cuts strikes a chord with many of my clients.
Well, let's see if you can buck the trend. I can see why there's no love lost between you and the big DIY companies, but you shouldn't concern yourself with them.

What changes to the website did you have in mind? The overriding factor in attracting more visitors to the site is to focus on keywords and links to other websites.

Let me know. Ready when you are.

Jake
___

Thanks for getting back to me so quickly, Jake.
I know what you mean about relevant keywords for Google and other search engines, but I'm not convinced by the "links to other websites" idea. Links often come with strings attached. What will these sites want from me in return? My customers, probably.

Also, we may need to look again at design and colour of the website. I've been *flicking through* some DIY brochures. Apart from the fact that they tend to be *littered with* spelling mistakes, they do present their products beautifully.

Maybe we should get together soon and I can show you what I mean.
Next Friday?
Regards

George
—

Great idea. Friday fine.
As you suggest, presentation is *the bottom line*.
 See you very soon.

Jake
—

TELEPHONE CONVERSATION BETWEEN MIDDLE-AGED BROTHER AND SISTER

ALISON: *Hello, little brother. It's me.*

STEVE: *Who's "me"?*

ALISON: *Your sister! Who do you think it is?*

STEVE: *Oh, sorry. I'm a little groggy this morning. I haven't got myself together yet.*

ALISON: *That's par for the course for you. Anything particularly wrong?*

STEVE: *Not really, no.*

ALISON: *What does "not really" mean?*

STEVE: *Well, Susan's just taken the kids to school in a huff.*

ALISON: *What did you do to get her going?*

STEVE: *How do you know it was me who annoyed her?*

ALISON: *Because you're my brother. I lived with you for 25 years, remember. My sister-in-law is very level-headed. She doesn't go off in a huff without good reason.*

STEVE: *You're* way off the mark *there. She shouts a lot and has a go at me for everything, especially in the mornings. Usually when she criticises the way I do things, I* take it on the chin, *but I wasn't up for it this morning. I'm clearly* <u>not</u> flavour of the month *in her books.*
Anyway, I'm fine. How are you?

ALISON: *OK, I suppose*

STEVE: *Now I have to ask you what I suppose means?*

ALISON: *Yes, you do.*

STEVE: *(sighs)…What does "I suppose" mean?*

ALISON: *Well, we're having a few problems with David's school. There are some nasty boys giving him a hard time.*

STEVE: *Bullying?*

ALISON: *That sort of thing, yes. Very unpleasant. I've been to see the Head about it, but she keeps trying to* duck the issue. *She's admitted that there are two boys in David's class that need* reining in, *and all she has promised to do is ask the Deputy Head to write a general report on school behaviour. It will be a total* whitewash, *I know. I could deal with the matter myself; I know who the boys are, but if I go and speak to their parents, it could make things worse for David and even lead to a* vicious circle *of pointless complaining and nasty responses.*

STEVE: *Or you could change schools? Send him somewhere which* ticks all the right boxes. The flip side *is that you could always teach him at home yourself.*

ALISON: *That's much easier said than done, as you well know. Anyway, his exams are* looming. *Too late to change now.*

STEVE: *You see, the problem of poor behaviour in our schools today has been caused by the* demise *of discipline and common courtesy in our society. As I've often said-*

ALISON: *Oh dear, what have I started? I don't want one of your lectures.*

STEVE: *Respect for others ought to be* enshrined in law-

ALISON: *And respect for your sister means you will understand that I have to go now. Kisses to the kids. Bye!*

STEVE: *Another woman leaving me* in a huff!

Chapter Seven: **Exercise**

CHOOSE THE CORRECT WORD FROM THOSE IN GREEN
Answers on page 140

1. A: *I'm feeling really* ᵃ*(level-headed/groggy/enshrined/whitewashed) this morning, and my mood has not been lifted by the dark skies I see* ᵇ*(enshrined/grumbling/mulling over/ looming) above.*
    B: *Oh stop* ᶜ*(ducking the issue/grumbling/flicking through/ticking all the right boxes), you whinger!*

2. *Freedom of speech is* ᵃ*(enshrined/mulled over/undercut/overridden) in our constitution. It is* ᵇ*(a whitewash/an overriding/an enshrining/a looming) human right, the* ᶜ*(brunt/bottom line/ demise/grumbling) of which will have a damaging effect on our society in this country.*

3. A: *The deal does look good on paper, but will undoubtedly* ᵃ*(be way off the mark/tick all the right boxes/be a whitewash/come with strings attached). It could also cause an unwelcome* ᵇ*(knock-on effect/brunt/flavour of the month/undercut) in that everybody else will want the same contract.*
    B: *I'll take the documents home and* ᶜ*(get the balls rolling/override them/flick through them/ duck the issue) tonight. Maybe I can come up with an alternative.*

4. *By refusing to panic and remaining* ᵃ*(groggy/level-headed/mulled over/in a huff), they have, unlike many of their competitors, managed to* ᵇ*(buck the trend/rein in/flick through/come with strings attached). They are clearly* c*(level-headed/in a vicious circle/the bottom line/ flavour of the month); everybody wants their products.*

5. A: *She should learn to take negative feedback* ᵃ*(in a huff/bucking the trend/on the chin/ as level-headed). There's no point in her going off* ᵇ*(in a huff/groggy/striking a chord/reining in) and sulking about it.*
    B: *Quite right. And later she should* ᶜ*(flick through/mull over/bear the brunt/grumble) what she has been told and focus on what she needs to do to improve.*

6. *All the newspapers at the moment are* ᵃ*(mulled over/bucking the trend/level-headed/littered with) depressing articles about the economic crisis in Europe. It appears that few governments have managed to* ᵇ*(override/bear the brunt/rein in/undercut) public sector spending.*

7. A: *There's clearly* ᵃ*(grumbling/a knock-on effect/no love lost/a flavour of the month) between them…and what she said about him was* ᵇ*(groggy/way off the mark/enshrined/bucking the trend).*
    B: *Actually, I don't agree. I can see what she means. It really* ᶜ*(got the ball rolling/loomed large/ticked all the right boxes/struck a chord) with me.*

8. *There are some deep-rooted problems here that we need to resolve. We can't keep on* ^a*(ducking the issue/striking a chord/flicking through/taking it on the chin). Can't you all see that?* ^b*(To get the ball rolling/The bottom line/To loom large/The flick side) is that unless we start to* ^c*(undercut/bear the brunt/whitewash/mull over) our competitors, we will lose our share of the market.*

9. *A: The judges' enquiry into the handling of Government military weapons contracts was an utter* ^a*(vicious circle/flick-through/knock-on effect/whitewash), don't you agree?*
   B: Indeed. ^b*(Way off the mark/Flavour of the month/Par for the course/The bottom line)! What did you expect? That the Ministry of Defence would have to* ^c*(get the ball rolling/bear the brunt/buck the trend/duck the issue) of an unfavourable ruling from the judiciary?*

10. *It's very important that you don't allow yourself to get into a* ^a*(vicious circle/huff/demise/whitewash) of negative thinking whereby you reject every idea that comes along just because it doesn't* ^b*(take it on the chin/buck the trend/come with strings attached/tick all the right boxes). Sooner or later you are going to have to* ^c*(strike a chord/get the ball rolling/rein it in/duck the issue).*

Lesson One

To take a swipe at (To make a negative comment about someone)

Examples:
- *He rarely misses the opportunity **to take a swipe at** me, but I never let myself rise to the bait.*
- *She **took a swipe at** him for stealing her thunder. He knew it was her idea but he tried to fob her off with pathetic excuses*

To overdo (To exaggerate, to go too far, to do too much--*sometimes used sarcastically to say that someone isn't doing much work at all. See first example below*.)

Examples:
- A: *What have you been up to today?*

  B: *I felt a bit groggy so I've spent all day flicking through newspapers and bingeing on chocolate.*

  A: *Sounds like par for the course for you. Don't **overdo** it, will you!*
- *You need to cook the potatoes for just ten minutes. But if you **overdo** them, it will have a knock-on effect on the rest of the meal.*

Credit where credit's due (Praise is given even though one doesn't want to give it)

Examples:
- *He has been an appalling goalkeeper for us and the supporters are right to take a swipe at him. But **credit where credit's due**, he played quite well today.*
- *She made far too many blunders when she was in office, but **credit where credit's due**, she never attempted to pass the buck.*

To delve into (To investigate deeply, to look into something in great detail)

Examples:
- *If you **delve into** his past, you will see that whenever he has been given free rein to work without restrictions, he has wreaked havoc.*
- *The bottom line is that I am not going to put up with anyone **delving into** my private life just to see if I tick all the right boxes.*

Sporadic (Occasional)

Examples:
- ***Sporadic*** *periods of sunshine is the weather forecast for today; I'm not sure it's worth going to the beach. I might as well stay in and plod on with my housework.*
- A: *Don't make any hasty decisions based on his advice. He only gets things right **sporadically**.*

  B: *No love lost between you two then?*

To take one's hat off to (To admire someone for a particular reason)

Examples:
- *Everyone thought his enquiry was going to be a whitewash, but he delved into the subject in great detail. I **take my hat off to** him.*
- *You've got to **take your hat off to** them. During the recession their business bucked the trend, and is still thriving today.*

To ring/sound alarm bells (To be a warning)

Examples:
- ***Alarm bells*** *should have **sounded** when we struggled to pay the first invoice, knowing full well that more of them were looming ahead. It should be a rule of thumb that we don't buy things we can't afford.*
- *When I spot a fresh-looking signature on a painting, **alarm bells** start to **ring**. It's almost certainly a fake.*

To demonize (To make someone seem a much worse person than in fact they are)

Examples:
- *She's been vilified and unfairly **demonized** in her home country, but over here in the UK it's the reverse. She's everybody's flavour of the month.*
- *It's no wonder he went off in a huff; you've **demonized** him all his adult life and you just can't resist taking a swipe at him whenever the opportunity arises. You'll get your just deserts one day.*

To cut off one's nose to spite one's face (To do something with the intention of harming another person, but which ends in harming oneself even more)

Examples:
- A: *Punishing and shouting at your children for misbehaviour can often end up with you **cutting off your nose to spite your face**. They usually take it on the chin, while you end up getting very upset with yourself for losing it with them.*

  B: *Yes, that very much strikes a chord with me.*
- A: *I'm going to force my husband to join me in sitting through an evening with my parents.*

  B: *Are you sure you wouldn't be **cutting off your nose to spite your face**? You know you always clash with your mum*

To fester (To get worse or more intense--*generally because action is not taken. It is often used with "allow/let"*)

Examples:
- *Alarm bells should have rung a long time ago. Don't <u>let</u> things **fester**. Get it out of your system now.*
- *She <u>allowed</u> the difficult issues she had with her boyfriend to **fester**, and he never gave her free rein to express herself. A recipe for disaster in a relationship.*

*"When I spot a fresh-looking signature on a painting, **alarm bells start to ring**. It's almost certainly a fake."*

(see page 108)

Lesson Two

To get short shrift from someone (To get a quick, angry and precise response from someone, so that one is left in no doubt how the speaker feels)

Examples:
- *The jury is still out on Juanito; he's only been a Premiership player for one season. But **I got short shrift from** his manager when I asked if the player was going to be replaced next season.*
- *You'll **get short shrift from** her if you suggest there's been a cover-up. I'd only mention it as a last resort if I were you.*

To tarnish (To discredit, to damage the reputation of someone/something)

Examples:
- A: *I'm really concerned that he is **tarnishing** the name of our company. He needs to be reined in.*
- B: *But credit where credit's due; he has clinched us same great deals this year. You don't want to cut off your nose to spite your face, do you?*
- *I understand why you want to appear younger to your fans, but don't overdo it. You will **tarnish** your image if you look ridiculous.*

To twiddle one's thumbs (To sit around doing nothing when you should be working, to have nothing to do)

Examples:
- *Business is sporadic at the moment. I've been moping around all day **twiddling my thumbs**. I'm on tenterhooks waiting for something to happen*
- A: *When I accused him of **twiddling his thumbs** instead of pulling his weight in the office, he didn't bat an eyelid.*
- B: *That doesn't bode well at all, does it?*

To slash (To reduce radically, to cut back)

Examples:
- *Our prices have been **slashed**. Flick through one of our brochures and see for yourselves.*

- *The Chancellor has been demonized in the press for stating that public expenditure has to be **slashed**. He has also given short shrift to anyone who has suggested this may cause another recession leading to further bank bail-outs.*

Overstretched (Stretched too far and therefore in short supply; asked to do too much)

Examples:
- *We cannot overlook the fact that funds are **overstretched** this quarter. But we should have confidence in our ability to turn things around, so let's not do ourselves down; things are bound to pick up in the not-too-distant future.*
- A: *Our own natural resources in this country are very much **overstretched**. It's a problem which every new Government promises to delve into. We are all craving a fresh political approach to the problem.*

  B: *Well, you're going to have to sit around twiddling your thumbs. This Government will be even worse than the previous one in failing to get things done; you wait and see.*
- *If you think you are being **overstretched** at work, say something to your boss. Don't let it fester.*

To sit on something (To fail to deal with something, to take too long in acting)

Examples:
- *Somebody needs to give him a dressing down. He's been **sitting on** this transaction for nearly six months. What's got into him?*
- *The minister has been shunning the limelight, no doubt having been made fully aware by his colleagues that he cannot continue to **sit on** this issue.*

To milk it/this (To extend and enjoy the celebration of success, to take all possible advantage of a situation for a long time--*an informal expression often used in sport*)

Examples:
- A: *He has never won Wimbledon before, so you can't blame him for **milking it**.*

  B: *I understand, but I still think he's overdoing it.*
- A: *I take my hat off to you guys. That was a stunning victory.*

  B: *Thanks; we're going **to milk this** for quite some time, I can assure you!*

To be in awe of someone (To treat someone as a hero, to feel small in the presence of someone perceived to be great)

Examples:

- As a young child she was always **in awe of** her elder brother, despite his nastiness towards her. She came to her senses, however, later on in life when he tried to rope her into his criminal activities.
- Great musicians have loomed very large in my life, and I've been **in awe of** each and every one of them. Pathetic, I know.

A: *"I'm really concerned that he is **tarnishing** the name of our company. He needs to be reined in.*

B: *But credit where credit's due; he has clinched us same great deals this year. You don't want to cut off your nose to spite your face, do you?"*

(see page 110)

To set in stone (To make something permanent--*similar to "enshrine", see earlier, page 98, but not limited to law, and often used in the negative. Note also the expression "to leave no stone unturned", which means to conduct a thorough and complete investigation into something*)

Examples:
- You know, <u>nothing</u>'s **set in stone**; if anyone wants to step in and change what I've done, that's fine by me. Nobody's going to close ranks in this company.
- There's no need to look so glum. We won't burden you with work you can't cope with and we certainly don't want you to feel that we are overstretching you. Your terms of reference are <u>not</u> **set in stone**, so we can play it by ear and see how it goes.
- The head of Channel TV3 has admitted that they took liberties in showing this very uncomplimentary programme about the Royal Family in the week of The Queen's Diamond Jubilee. He promised **to leave no stone unturned** in his search to unravel exactly what went on. It won't be a whitewash, he claimed.

Stance (The attitude of a person or organization towards something--*often used with "tough"*)

Examples:
- The Labour Party has recently changed its **stance** <u>on</u> immigration to the UK. It's a problem that was allowed to fester during their governing years. It's interesting to see that now they are in opposition, they no longer try to demonize members of the current Government as racists when they mention that alarm bells concerning immigration should have sounded many years ago.
- We will take a **tough stance against** anyone who attempts to tarnish the reputation of this firm. We won't stand for it.

Lesson Three

Hunch (An instinctive feeling about what is going to happen)

Examples:
- *It's just a **hunch**, but I think that jobs in this industry are going to be slashed and that we in administration will bear the brunt.*
- *The **hunch** she had that Peter would set the ball rolling, and new plans for the business would soon be unveiled, was right. I take my hat off to her for being spot-on with her predictions.*

To rant, a rant (To complain loudly and for too long; a long speech of complaint, either written or spoken, that never seems to end)

Examples:
- *It's no good **ranting** at me for not taking a tough stance against him. He always goes off in a huff whenever I try talking to him.*
- *This article in The Times is a bit of **a rant** against the previous Prime Minister. It vilifies him for having acted too hastily in taking the country to war, but it's easy to criticise in hindsight.*

To take someone to task for/over something (To criticise/tell someone off for their mistake)

Examples:
- *We **took the directors to task for** spending money when we were already overstretched. They're all fat cats who wouldn't even notice if the odd million pounds goes astray.*
- *If you're going **to take him to task over** why he acted so recklessly, make sure he doesn't attempt to duck any questions.*

Watershed

i. (A crucial turning point, a moment that changes everything for the future)
Examples:
- A: *My life had been in disarray until I started this fantastic job. It was a real **watershed** moment for me. I had squandered many years drifting with no sense of purpose. Now my stance on life has changed. Crack open the champagne!*
- B: *Don't overdo it!*

- *I have been left somewhat bereft of hope. I had a hunch that the meeting was going to mark a **watershed** in our negotiations with the bank. How wrong I was*

ii. (A time of day before which programmes that are unsuitable for children should not be shown on television)
Example:
- *I know it sounds like a typical parental rant, but I do think this programme should be on after the 9pm **watershed**, don't you?*
- *The BBC will tarnish its spotless reputation if it puts on this film before the **watershed**.*

Shrinking violet (Someone who is very shy and afraid to speak--*often used in the negative as an understatement. See first example below*)

Examples:
- A: *He'll get short shrift from her if he tries telling her his corny jokes.*
  B: *Yes, she's <u>no</u> **shrinking violet** is she? She'll let him know exactly what she thinks of him.*
- *My dad, despite his shortcomings, has an outgoing personality. My mum, on the other hand, tends to keep tight-lipped about things and is a bit of a **shrinking violet** when in company.*

To pay lip service to (To say something but not actually do it properly, to give support verbally but not in actions--*a negative expression*)

Examples:
- A: *Successive governments in my country have merely **paid lip service to** the armed forces. When it comes to the crunch, there is a stark contrast between what they say and what they do.*
  B: *Do you think my country is any different? All governments throughout the western world are much of a muchness.*
- *My daughter's school **pays lip service to** sport. Flipping through the brochure, designed to allure sporty girls to the school, one sees many beautiful photos of girls playing sport. But I can tell you, as a parent of a girl at the school, they hardly do any.*

To allude to, allusion (To refer to something indirectly, to touch on something--see ***Advanced Everyday English***, *page 46–an indirect reference to something*)

Examples:
- *You **alluded to** this last time we spoke. Have you now changed your stance on religious education?*
- *Her speech was littered with **allusions** to the comments she previously made relating to the demise of the British Empire.*

To plough (back) into (To (re)invest large sums of money--*usually governments and large companies*)

Examples:
- *The new Government have promised **to plough back into** the National Health Service the vast sums of money that were squandered on non-medical professional services. I am mindful, however, that political promises are never set in stone.*
- *The shareholders have opted not to take a dividend this year, but instead **to plough** the company's profits **back into** the business. I don't mind, but the directors seem to be twiddling their thumbs and are just sitting on it.*

To fly in the face of (To go against an assumption, generally accepted philosophy or rules and regulations)

Examples:
- *I have to take you to task on these new rules, which I hope aren't set in stone. They **fly in the face of** everything we've striven for in this firm for over 50 years.*
- *Slashing funds for the arts in this country **flies in the face of** modern intellectual thought on cultural education for the young. Politicians often only pay lip service to these matters.*

To unravel

i. (To solve a mystery)
Examples:
- *Alarm bells started to ring when the police began to **unravel** the strange goings-on in the village.*
  (see picture below)
- *The real cause of his death will never be **unravelled** by this whitewash of an enquiry.*

ii. (To begin to fall apart, go wrong--*generally someone's story or efforts to do something*)
Example:
- *The more the prosecution lawyer delved into his past, the more his defence began to **unravel**. Deep down, he knew he didn't have a leg to stand on.*
- *As her attempts to make amends for having squandered all their savings **unravelled**, he got on his high horse about it and went off in a huff.*

PRIME MINISTER'S SPEECH TO STUDENTS

Good evening everybody.

It's lovely to see so many people here tonight. Thank you for coming. I'd love to tell you that all is rosy in the garden of our country…but that would get short shrift from *you clever young people. There are many economic problems we need to face up to, not just in our country, but the world as a whole. Letting them* fester *will not help us in the long run.*

I know lots of you blame the bankers for the crisis we are in. In many ways you are right; too many of them have only thought of short-term profit. But it would be quite wrong to demonize *them, even though we all feel like having a* rant. *This country has a long banking tradition stretching back hundreds of years. A large proportion of our tax revenue comes from the banks, which is then* ploughed back into *the public sector. If my Government introduces tight regulations on what banks can and cannot do, we will scare away investors. It would be* cutting off our nose to spite our face.

However, the banks do need to be taken to task over *the bonus culture, which pays individuals ludicrous sums of money, when capital funds are* overstretched. *This is a problem that my cabinet are not simply going to* sit on. *We will be presenting our plans for change in the next few weeks. At the same time, we must all take a good look at ourselves and ask why* alarm bells *didn't* ring *sooner during the good times.*

The last Prime Minister sold off many of our assets and then spent the money on expensive, flawed projects. I take my hat off *to those emerging countries, like China, that have saved huge amounts of money. We now reluctantly have to rely on their help. The Chancellor* alluded to *this last week when he was interviewed on the radio. He said, "The East weren't just sitting there* twiddling their thumbs *while countries in the West were having to* slash *their spending budgets to deal with their deficits. "But now is not the time to* delve into *the issues of East versus West.*

You would like, I imagine, to hear more about our plans for your futures. Yes, I know you all want to take a swipe at *me for raising tuition fees at our universities. I understand why you may feel that way. But remember, every single politician in the House of Commons, no matter what side of the political divide they are from, would have done the same in my position. Without this extra money going into higher education, some universities would have to close and many others would lose their world-class reputations. This* flies in the face of *common sense.*

There is, however, light at the end of the tunnel, I can assure you. Nothing is set in stone, *which is why I like to take a flexible approach to dealing with all problems. When I travel abroad, I am constantly amazed and flattered by the praise I receive from foreign leaders on behalf of our country… and virtually everyone is* in awe of *our wonderful Royal Family. The current turmoil in the world economy marks a* watershed *in our shared histories. Unfortunately, many of our dreams formed over the last*

50 years of prosperity are unravelling.

It pains me that you, the young, have to bear the brunt of so much hardship. You may think that my Government is in disarray, but I am a stickler for getting things right. Please have faith in me.
Now, any questions from the audience?

FOOTBALL CORRESPONDENT ON TV NEWS

NEWSREADER: *And now for sports news. In case some of you think you have been dreaming, I can confirm that England have won the World Cup. They have beaten Brazil 1-0. Let's speak to Chris, who is live in Moscow outside the stadium. Chris, can you believe it?*

CORRESPONDENT: *Hi Monica. Well, it is unbelievable, isn't it? It's just beginning to sink in. I had a* hunch *we were going to do it. To be fair, we didn't play that well, but* credit where credit's due, *the boys never gave up, never stopped believing they could do it. Both teams only attacked* sporadically, *but the England manager brought on an extra striker 20 minutes from the end, and that made the difference.*

NEWSREADER: *And how have the fans reacted?*

CORRESPONDENT: *Well, they've all been* milking it *and will be doing so for quite some time, as you can imagine. Who can blame them?*
On a sad note, there is one thing that has tarnished *the final and the World Cup as a whole: racist abuse by so-called football fans of our black and mixed- race players. It's an absolute disgrace and FIFA really has to take a* tough stance against *this unacceptable behaviour by what appears to be large sections of the crowd. It's not just a small minority. Every time this sort of thing happens, the idiots who run world football merely* pay lip service to *what we have achieved in the UK, but nothing seems to change on the international stage. I've got a bee in my bonnet about it, as you know, Monica. Anyway, let's put this to one side for now. We've won the World Cup, Monica! We've done it!*

NEWSREADER: *Now don't you go* overdoing *it, will you Chris?*

CORRESPONDENT: *And you're no* shrinking violet *yourself when it comes to celebrating…so I've been led to believe .*

NEWSREADER: *(Jokingly) I resent that remark! I will be consulting my lawyer.*
Enjoy the rest of the evening, Chris. I think you're in for a long night.

Chapter Eight: **Exercise**

CHOOSE THE CORRECT WORD FROM THOSE IN GREEN
Answers on page 140

1.   A: *Many theatre critics love to* ᵃ*(take a tough stance against him/take a swipe at him/cut off his nose to spite his face/fester him), but I think he's the best actor this country has ever produced. He's absolutely amazing.*
    B: ᵇ*(Milking it/Demonizing him/Credit where credit's due/Nothing is set in stone), but don't* ᶜ*(overdo/fester/allude/delve into)it.*

2.   A: *By continuing to* ᵃ*(rant/hunch/demonize/tarnish) on and on and on about the same thing and not allow Daniel to go out with his friends, you are* ᵇ*(taking everyone to task/setting it in stone/cutting off your nose to spite your face/sounding alarm bells). You will be the one who ends up suffering the most.*
    B: *So you think I should just let the problem* ᶜ*(tarnish/fester/plough back/unravel,), do you*

3.   *It was most enlightening* ᵃ*(paying lip service to/alluding to/flying in the face of/delving into) her past as a young politician. She was no* ᵇ*(shrinking violet/hunch/watershed/thumb twiddler), that's for sure. She certainly stood up for what she believed in. I* ᶜ*(pay lip service to/take a tough stance against/take my hat off to/delve into)her.*

4.   *The Employment Minister assured those present that the Government will* ᵃ*(allude to/take a tough stance against/take their hats off to/delve into) benefit cheats. Previous administrations have only* ᵇ*(paid lip service to/flown in the face of/got short shrift from/overdone) dealing with such matters. People who make no effort to find work and live off the Welfare State deserve to be* ᶜ*(sporadic/delved into/ploughed back/demonized) in my opinion.*

5.   A: *I got* ᵃ*(lip service/a hunch/short shrift/a watershed) from the Chancellor when I asked him why money received from raised taxes had not been* ᵇ*(overstretched/ploughed back/delved/alluded) into the National Health Service.*
    B: *Par for the course, really. Who do these politicians think they are? They expect us all to be* ᶜ*(in awe of/demonized by/tarnished by/alluded to) them. Not me!*

6.   A: *I'm not sure how much work has been done on this. They're probably in their offices just* ᵃ*(milking it/taking their hats off/overdoing it/twiddling their thumbs).*
    B: *Most likely. We really should* ᵇ*(ring alarm bells/get short shrift/take them to task/take a tough stance against them) on why they have been* ᶜ*(sitting on/milking/delving into/festering) this matter for so long.*

7.   *He keeps* ᵃ*(sitting on/alluding to/taking a swipe at/flying in the face of)* his mistaken belief that funds at the club to buy new players are ᵇ*(overstretched/demonized/ tarnished/taken to task).* This ᶜ*(takes a tough stance against/sits on/is in awe of/flies in the face of)* reality. The club has more money than it knows what to do with.

8.	A: *Their success in this tournament over the years has been somewhat* [a](*demonized/ overdone/sporadic/ploughed back,*) *so it's not surprising they are* [b](*setting it in stone/alluding to it/paying lip service to it/milking it*).
	B: *Indeed. And I have a* [c](*rant/hunch/slash/twiddle*) *that it will be a very long time before they win anything else again.*

9.	*His claims about his being a moral member of society started to* [a](*unravel/be overstretched/ fly in the face/fester*) *when journalists put him on the spot by asking him questions about his private life. This later proved to be a* [b](*hunch/rant/watershed/sporadic*) *moment for him. Since then, his image as a model husband and father has been severely* [c](*unravelled/ slashed/alluded/tarnished*).

10.	A: *I suppose* [a](*credit where credit's due/alarm bells should have rung/it was a watershed/a tough stance was taken*) *when a couple of older workers were laid off last year. But I would never have expected half the workforce to be* [b](*slashed/unravelled/milked/overstretched*) *over such a short space of time.*
	B: *I know. You think you have a job for life, but this just goes to show that* [c](*credit where credit's due/ you shouldn't cut off your nose to spite your face/nothing is set in stone/ you should take a tough stance*).

Lesson One

To rest on one's laurels (To be complacent because of what one has achieved in the past--*for "complacent "see **Advanced Everyday English**, page 44*)

Examples:
- *We are truly flattered by some of the complimentary remarks made about our services, particularly those that have highlighted how we are bucking the trend when many of our competitors are feeling the pinch. But we can't afford **to rest on our laurels**.*
- *I think my worries about what could happen if he **rested on his laurels** have been vindicated. The economic recession has clearly taken its toll on his business.*

To blend in (To go well together, particularly with other colours in a pattern, to fit in--*see **Practical Everyday English**, page 69*--to look so natural and comfortable with a new group of people that one doesn't stand out as being new to the group)

Examples:
- *It's a stunning picture. I especially admire the way Monet makes the green leaves of the trees **blend in** with the background of blue sky.*
- A: *I don't think she's a fake. She genuinely **blends in** with the rest of the girls in the office.*
- B: *I'm not so sure. I think she's going to ruffle a few feathers around here.*

Entrenched (Firmly held/established--*used to describe opinions, beliefs, customs and traditions, which are difficult to change*)

Examples:
- *He is very set in his ways and his **entrenched** views on the role of women in society fly in the face of modern thinking.*
- *Excessive red tape is very much **entrenched** in my country's local politics. Trying to get anything done quickly here can be quite an ordeal… like banging your head against a brick wall, actually.*

To agree to disagree (To accept amicably that one can't agree on a particular matter)

Examples:
- She thought that the whole thing was done and dusted and that her ex-husband had finally come to his senses. But in the end they had **to agree to disagree** on a few issues.
- A: I think, John, we'll have **to agree to disagree** on this one.
  B: Most probably right. Let's plod on.

To gloat (To show off and make people feel inferior for having lost/failed or not done so well, to talk about another person's misfortunes with satisfaction because one is more fortunate--*often used in informal/non-serious situations*)

Examples:
- A: So, how does it feel to be bottom of the league?
  B: Stop **gloating**! Our only problem was that we peaked too early.
  A: By winning one match at the beginning of the season? I suppose cheaper tickets next season in Division 2 might soften the blow a bit.
- Head teacher:
  We don't want to **gloat** or rest on our laurels, but the school has once again lived up to its reputation as being the finest in London. I offer my commiserations to other schools that are clearly not up to scratch.
  One pupil quietly to another:
  Isn't that **gloating**?

Half-hearted (Not fully committed, lacking enthusiasm--*often used with "attempt"*)

Examples:
- A: Can I just chip in and say some of the directors have only made a **half-hearted** attempt to address the problem?
  B: Yes, I agree; heads should roll.
- If you had stuck to your guns and taken the bull by the horns, you might have clinched the deal, but in the end you failed to bowl them over. Why was your approach so **half-hearted**?

*"It's a stunning picture. I especially admire the way Monet makes the green leaves of the trees **blend in** with the background of blue sky."* *(see page 122)*

Not to hold your breath (Not to expect something to happen anytime soon)

Examples:

- A: *I know she has many shortcomings, but when she says she's going to do something, it will get done…often in the nick of time.*

  B: *I **wouldn't hold your breath**!*

- *He admits he has squandered most of their savings and has been reckless with money all his life. He claims now that he will be turning over a new leaf very shortly. **Don't hold your breath!***

To gloss over (To deal with an issue only superficially and therefore not talk deeply enough about it)

Examples:
- A: *We'll just have to agree to disagree.*
  B: *No I don't think that's right. You're just **glossing over** the subject because you don't want to come to terms with reality.*
- *The Chancellor pays lip service to his economic advisers. His latest speech merely **glossed over** the very deep financial concerns facing the country at the moment.*

To dig one's heels in (Not to give up until one gets what one wants--*note also the expression "**to drag one's heels**", which means to take too long in coming to a decision and getting something done*)

Examples:
- *Everyone else might have a half-hearted attitude, but I'm going to **dig my heels in**. This is not something that should be glossed over.*
- *Those old men have got very entrenched views on how to go about doing things. You're going to have **to dig your heels in** if you want to change their mindset. I know you're no shrinking violet, so I'm sure you won't hold back.*
- A: *I don't know why the Government are **dragging their heels** over this matter. It's an excellent opportunity to plough some money back into British farming. What do you think is going on?*
  B: *Red tape.*

To go off the rails (To lose one's way in life--*often because of excessive or addictive behaviour, e.g. alcohol, drugs, gambling etc.*)

Examples:
- *It's true; he does have a big chip on his shoulder. But I do feel so desperately sorry that he's **gone off the rails** with his relentless drinking. Nobody has a right to gloat.*
- *Her story began to unravel when her own lawyer, in a half-hearted attempt to gain sympathy form the jury, alluded to the fact that her life **went off the rails** when she turned to drugs and gambling. It got short shrift, though, from the prosecuting barrister.*

Chapter Nine

Lesson Two

To muddle up (To mix up, confuse things--*note also the expression "to muddle through", which means to manage to do something, but with difficulty and little skill*)

Examples:

- *Instead of just sitting there twiddling your thumbs, take this coffee to your dad and hot chocolate to your brother... and don't **muddle them up**.*
  (see picture below)
- A: *I got all **muddled up** with the dates. I thought your parents were coming this Saturday and we were seeing Pete and Jane the following weekend.*
  B: *Very much par for the course. You're looking very bleary-eyed. You could do with an early night, I think.*
- *I'm feeling a bit groggy this morning and my wife went off in a huff over something trivial. I've also got a lot of things on my plate at work. But I suppose I'll just have **to muddle through** somehow.*

To find wanting (To discover that something is not good enough/lacking in necessary quality--*often discovered after investigation--usually used in the passive voice, see 2nd example below*)

Examples:
- *The Chemistry Department is going to bear the brunt of job cuts. We **found it wanting** in many areas, and their claim to be at the cutting edge of science education was way off the mark.*
- *As far as I can see, most Members of Parliament have only made a half-hearted attempt to change their ways since the expenses scandal came to light a few years ago. And I have to say that in almost every avenue we looked down they <u>were</u> **found wanting**.*

Smug (Too self-satisfied--*note that "smug" is stronger and more negative than "complacent"*-see *Advanced Everyday English*, page 44- and "**to rest on one's laurels**"-see earlier *page 122*. A "smug" person wants to show the world he is self-satisfied*)

Examples:
- *There's no need to gloat…and you can wipe that **smug** smile off your face too. I know you deserved to win but I don't want to hear you go on about it.*
- *I won't allow myself to rise to his bait; he can be as **smug** as he likes, but his sneering manner really does take the biscuit.*

To wince (To show pain in one's facial expression--*often because of embarrassment as a result of seeing/hearing something unpleasant--note also the verb "**to squirm**" which is to show acute discomfort at something embarrassing or shameful. It is more emphatic than "to wince", but very similar in meaning*)

Examples:
- *My husband **winced** when our son's teacher told us his maths this year had been found wanting. He won't be able to just muddle through next year, that's for sure.*
- *I **winced** when I realised my wife was going to dig her heels in until she got the medication she wanted. The doctor nearly walked out of the surgery. I don't blame him.*
- *You may think that resorting to nasty tactics could be cutting off my nose to spite my face, especially if the press start telling their readers that I'm not such a nice bloke. But I really want to see him **squirm** in court when my lawyer puts him on the spot.*

To fend for   (To provide a living--*note also "**to fend off**" which means to repel/ fight off, often against minor contagious illnesses*)

Examples:

- *I think the penny has finally dropped. His parents are feeling the pinch and at 27 years old he will have **to fend for** <u>himself</u>. I have a hunch that he will do well.*
- *The doctor believes mum's earache is just a red herring, but her inability **to fend off** low grade viral infections is a source of worry. He has promised to leave no stone unturned.*

To lap up (To enjoy thoroughly, to love watching or listening to something/someone)

Examples:

- *Everything the Prime Minister says flies in the face of what his predecessors believed in, but the public just **lap it up**. I just wince every time I hear his voice.*
- *His holy ranting didn't go down so well in the UK, but they'll **lap him up** in the US, where strict religious views on life and society are more entrenched.*

Few and far between   (Not very often, not many-- *generally used in a negative sense i.e. complaining that something does not happen very often*)

Examples:

- *Patrick's visits to his mother over the past year have been **few and far between**. I think it's deplorable, especially when the rest of the family have rallied round her, poor soul.*
- A: *Real customers who actually come into the shop and purchase things rather than browse and then buy online are **few and far between**, unfortunately. It's a problem I wish I could simply gloss over… and perhaps business will pick up soon.*

  B: *Don't hold your breath.*

To have a word with someone
(To speak to someone, usually in private, about an important matter--*sometimes to tell that person off in a polite and calm way. So, if someone says, "I want to have a word with you"…it's probably going to be something you don't want to hear. Be warned!*)

Examples:
- Priest:
  *Mrs Smith, **can I have a word** (with you)? Your visits to Sunday Mass have been few and far between lately.*
- Lawyer's office:
  *The boss **had a word with** John about his sitting on far too many cases which are due to come to court very soon. With so many people in the office away at the moment, we are a bit overstretched, and I thought the boss was wrong to take John to task over it, I really do.*

To weather the storm
(To deal successfully with a set of problems over a period of time--note also the expression "***to go down a storm***", which means to be well received, to go down very well indeed--see **Practical Everyday English**, page 31)

Examples:
- *The Chancellor's recent budget was found wanting in some areas, but most political commentators believe he will **weather the storm** of criticism he has received.*
- *It will be interesting to see whether the Board of Directors will be able to **weather the storm**. They are certainly going to get short shrift from many of the shareholders.*
- *Everybody in the US seems to be in awe of the British Prime Minister. He **went down a storm** in the US Senate and is now milking it for every second he is away from the UK, many of whose citizens think he has gone off the rails.*

To outclass
(To be much better than others--*often used in sport and in the passive voice--note also "**to outshine**", which is very similar in meaning, but perhaps less emphatic*)

Examples:
- *I wince when I look at our defence. We were, once again, totally **outclassed** by Barcelona, and my wife, who comes from that region of Spain, was absolutely lapping it up.*
- *He was **outshone** by his smug brother at school while he muddled through and later had to fend for himself.*

Lesson Three

To get one's act together (To concentrate and start doing things properly after a period of disorganisation, to organise oneself)

Examples:
- *Actually, I must admit that I've been dragging my heels a bit on this problem. Time for me **to get my act together**; otherwise all hell will break loose.*
- *We cannot afford to rest on our laurels. Nothing is set in stone. Alarm bells are beginning to ring, so we must **get our act together** now for the sake of the business.*

Sluggish (Very slow moving, inactive--*especially in business/the economy*--lacking in energy--*particularly after a poor night's sleep*)

Examples:
- *It is perhaps understandable that rich bankers are demonized by those who are not so well-off, but to blame them 100% for the current **sluggish** economy is way off the mark.*
- *I take my hat off to you. I don't know how you manage to be so bright and cheerful after the booze binge we went on last night. I'm feeling so **sluggish** this morning. I can't get my act together at all.*

Root and branch reform (A complete overhaul--*see earlier, **page 23**--Usually of a government department or public body/organisation; often used with "to carry out"*)

Examples:
- *The bottom line is that there has to be **root and branch reform** of the police. They don't deserve to be vilified, but it's galling to see such a decline in standards in recent years.*
- *The Prime Minister has promised to carry out **root and branch reform** of the taxation system. It clearly has many shortcomings, and new ideas need to be unveiled.*

To click/gel (To get on very well together--*people*--; to take shape, to begin to work well)

Examples:
- *I don't particularly want to delve into why we never* **clicked.** *Credit where credit's due, though; she didn't allow any resentment she may have had towards me to fester. In the end we just agreed to disagree on nearly everything.*
- A: *He just ticked all the right boxes and we really* **gelled** *from the very start.*

    B: *Oh dear, I can see a wedding looming!*

    A: *I wouldn't hold your breath!*
- *John had pulled me up on nearly everything I suggested. We were all in a bit of disarray and then, out of the blue, it all* **clicked** *into place; we decided to do away with the entire computing system and replace it with something much more up to date. We have already set the ball rolling.*

    (See picture below)

"I could have sworn" ("I'm almost certain that"--_often used when someone is surprised that he has forgotten to do or didn't do something, used informally_)

Examples:

- **I could have sworn** I left my keys here. I'm usually such a stickler for knowing where I put things. I must be losing the plot.
- A: I'm not trying to pass the buck here, but **I could have sworn** I gave you the documents yesterday.
  B: Oh, that's par for the course: you blaming others. I wasn't even here yesterday.

To get worked up about/over (To get annoyed and anxious about something--_also note the expressions "to work up enthusiasm", which means to get enthusiastic, generally used in the negative, and "to work up an appetite", which means to become hungry after a period of time_)

Examples:

- A: How someone so bereft of brains could be promoted to Divisional Manager in this company beggars belief. I can't cope with his gloating.
  B: **Don't get so worked up about** it. Your time will come. You will never be outshone by any of your colleagues.
- It's a very petty matter, not worth **getting worked up over.** We're all in the same boat anyway, and we'll come through this together.
- Andrew keeps trying to rope me into coming to local neighbourhood meetings. But to tell the truth, I find it difficult **to work up** any enthusiasm. There's too much red tape in local politics and I really can't be bothered.
- When I'm in Spain with my Spanish wife and kids, I try to go with the flow and eat late, as they do. But lunch at 3pm is taking the biscuit. I have usually **worked up** such an appetite by 1pm that I'd eat anything - even bull's testicles! And I don't want it to sound like a rant, but having dinner at 10pm is utterly ridiculous too.

To tick over (To keep going and survive, but not to make any money--_used in business/work_)

Examples:

- A: How's business?
  B: I mustn't grumble, **ticking over**… just about weathering the storm, I suppose. We've certainly got our work cut out, though.

- *Unfortunately, we are not in a position to plough back into the business the profit we made last year because this year we are only **ticking over**. I do wince a bit when I look at the accounts, I have to say.*

To pander to (To please people by doing something they want even if you don't believe it will serve their long term interest--*often used in politics*)

Examples:
- *In her latter years as Prime Minister, she fell from grace with her once adoring public because she refused **to pander to** their short-sighted desires. Her Government, however, bore the brunt of their displeasure and lost the following election.*
- *The problem with the previous Headmaster is that he **pandered** too much to the older members of staff, most of whom should have called it a day a long time ago. Everything he said struck a chord with them. The new Head, however, is much more level-headed, and has carried out root and branch reform of every academic department and all school policies.*

The tip of the iceberg (One small problem which can be seen amongst many much bigger ones that cannot)

Examples:
- *We are certainly not out of the woods yet. A long way from it, in fact. Raising the taxes of the well-off will not mean that the Government will have sufficient funds to bail out more banks and industries in the future. These issues relating to the tax rate of high earners are only **the tip of the iceberg**.*
- *It's just **the tip of the iceberg**, I'm afraid. The media is going to have a field day questioning the Home Secretary on her new policies to tackle juvenile crime. Some of us in her own party feel that her superficial comments do not bode well for the future. We are all waiting on tenterhooks for something more substantial to come from her lips.*

To count one's blessings (To be thankful for what one has and not to complain about what one doesn't have)

Examples:

- Husband and Wife:

  W: *Reading between the lines, I can see Peter and Kate are not happy. They clash over everything, even petty things.*

  H: *Indeed they do. You should **count your blessings** that you have me as a husband.*

- *Getting this job during such hard economic times is a real godsend. It has had a positive knock-on-effect for the whole family. We are all **counting our blessings**.*

To pan out (To end up, to turn out well--*see Practical Everyday English, page 49*)

Examples:

- *I'm not sure how it's all going **to pan out**. The problem you mention is just the tip of the iceberg. I suppose we should count our blessings and not get too worked up about it.*

- A: *I could have sworn he told me that the business was ticking over nicely with his new partners.*

  B: *He was just putting on a brave face. It's not really **panning out** at all.*

HEADMISTRESS'S SPEECH AT SCHOOL OPEN DAY

Good morning children and parents.

Welcome to St. Anne's Senior School for Girls. I want to say a few words about the school before some of our girls take you round the classrooms.

We are an unashamedly academic school and are very proud to have the finest exam results in the country. That is what the Sunday Times says about us. However, we don't want to rest on our laurels, and I certainly won't allow our staff or the girls to gloat or feel smug about our success. We have achieved such a fine record in recent times not by trying to outclass our competitors, but by carrying out root and branch reform in our teaching methods. To be honest, when I arrived at the school seven years ago, I soon became aware of an entrenched apathy towards raising standards. Things were just ticking over. Even our sports teams were only making half-hearted attempts to win matches. I thought to myself that I could either not make too much fuss and just blend in with my new surroundings, or I could dig my heels in. And good news for you: I chose the latter.

I'm not for one moment claiming that the change is all down to me. I'm just a catalyst. The hard work has been done by my amazing team of department heads and the brilliant Deputy Head, Brian Cole. He has left no stone unturned, I can assure you. When looking into how things might be improved at the school, he found a lot wanting and could have quite easily glossed over the problems he encountered, but instead he decided just muddling through wasn't good enough for St. Anne's. And it has all panned out beautifully. To put it bluntly, ladies and gentlemen, the school has really got its act together.

The girls are so happy here. It's fun to come to school every day. Many of them tell me how they gelled with their new classmates on the very first day. That's so heart-warming for me to hear. And when they get to school in the mornings, even though they may be feeling a bit sluggish, we start the day with a quick run around the playground followed by a healthy snack. The girls lap it up, don't you girls?

Well, there we are. I expect you're all getting quite fed up hearing me go on, so now it's time to see for yourselves.

Thank you so much for your time and enjoy your morning here at St. Anne's

BILL: *Hello Jim, how nice to see you. It's been a long time.*

JIM: *Hi Bill. It has indeed. I haven't been to this park for quite a while. I've been taking the dog to the forest. She loves it up there.*

BILL: *I could have sworn I saw you here yesterday with your dog, Trudy.*

JIM: *Well it wasn't me; you must have got me muddled up with another handsome fellow… and my dog's name is Patsy.*

BILL: *Oh dear. I think I need to have a word with my doctor. My eyesight and memory are getting worse.*

JIM: *It happens to all of us, Bill. But I have to say you're looking pretty fit to me.*

BILL: *Thanks Jim. Yes I suppose I should count my blessings at my age. I should be grateful that I can walk the dog every day. Mind you, I do wince a bit every time I get to the top of this hill. Anyway, enough of my whingeing. How are you and the family?*

JIM: *Oh, muddling through, I suppose. My two boys have left university. David is fending for himself, as I knew he would. And Joshua… well… he's gone off the rails a bit. Too much of the high life at university, I think. He says he's going to start looking for work, but I'm not holding my breath. Josh and I have learnt to agree to disagree on many issues, shall we say. But I still get worked up about his laziness. And how are things with you, Jim? I remember last time we met you were a bit concerned about whether your business was going to weather the storm.*

BILL: *I was right to worry. The problems we were having then were just the tip of the iceberg. Now clients, even local ones, are few and far between. I have probably paid the price for not pandering to the tastes of a younger market. But do you know what Jim? I'm really not bothered. I've lapped up the good times, put money away… and am thoroughly enjoying taking the dog out on a bright morning and bumping into you.*

JIM: *Likewise, Bill. Hope to see you tomorrow… weather permitting.*

CHOOSE THE CORRECT WORD FROM THOSE IN GREEN
Answers on page 140

1. *Even though we've done well this year, we can't afford to* ^a(*weather the storm/get worked up/rest on our laurels/blend in*) *and be complacent. If the economic climate worsens, there's no guarantee that we will be able to* ^b(*lap it up/weather the storm/gel/agree to disagree*). *I have a hunch that business opportunities next year will be* ^c(*few and far between/ entrenched/muddled up/the tip of the iceberg*).

2. A: *There's no point denying it; we were totally* ^a(*clicked/glossed over/gloated/outclassed*) *by Real Madrid today.*
    B: *We were, but some of our team don't help themselves by only making a* ^b(*smug/half-hearted/blended/winced*) *effort.*
    A: *And our goalkeeper was really* ^c(*gloating/gelling/pandering/found wanting*), *which didn't help.*

3. H: *You know: I'm such a wonderful husband. You should really be* ^a(*counting your blessings/ getting worked up/getting your act together/blending in*). *Many men I know have* ^b(*lapped it up/fended for themselves/gone off the rails/gloated*).
    W: *Excuse me if I* ^c(*click/wince/muddle through/dig my heels in*) *every time you open your mouth…Or maybe I should laugh?*

4. A: *Witty banter at work is* ^a(*winced/lapped up/gloated/entrenched*) *in British culture. It's something we believe helps staff to* ^b(*fend for themselves/gel /get worked up/tick over*).
    B: *I'm afraid we'll have to* ^c(*agree to disagree/muddle through/gloat/pan out*). *As a foreigner working in London, I don't know when people are joking and when they are being serious. Very frustrating!*

5. *I'm grateful that the business is at least* ^a(*half-hearted/lapping it up/ticking over/smug*) *in these difficult times. I can't complain. I hope we can continue* ^b(*getting worked up/ pandering/muddling/muddling through*) *next year. However, I do feel that there are major issues confronting us that we cannot afford to* ^c(*agree to disagree/gloat/gloss over/go off the rails*).

6. A: *I* ^a(*muddled up/could have sworn/panned out/glossed over*) *it was Friday today.*
    B: *I wish it was! You really do need to* ^b(*get your act together/muddle up/click/weather the storm*) *today. Why not try to be like me? I'm so well organized.*
    A: *And* ^c(*smug/entrenched/sluggish/outclassed*) *too!*

7. Once my daughter ^a(goes off the rails/gets her act together/laps it up/digs her heels in) about something, it's very difficult to change her way of thinking. My husband let's himself get so ^b(worked up/pandered/sluggish/entrenched) about this trait of hers. I really think he needs to ^c(outclass/have a word with/agree to disagree/blend in) her about it.

8. A: *She would prefer to sing her new songs but she* ^a*(gloats over/blends in/panders to/ fends for) her audiences and just sticks to her old classic hits. They just* ^b*(weather the storm/wince/ count their blessings/lap it up) and keep asking for more.*
    B: *Not me. I get all her songs* ^c*(muddled up/panned out/found wanting/worked up). They all sound the same to me.*

9. A: *When your kids go off to university, you worry if they are going to be able to* ^a*(lap up/ fend for themselves/go off the rails/tick over). Will they* ^b*(outclass/gloat/blend in/gloss over) with the other students or will they stick out like sore thumbs?*
    B: *You never know. You just have to wait and see how it all* ^c*(pans out/gels/panders/muddles up).*

10. A: *The problem of whether or not the police should be allowed to carry guns is just* ^a*(the storm being weathered/half-hearted/smug/the tip of the iceberg). The Government need to carry out* ^b*(root and branch reform/tip of the iceberg/a counting of one's blessings/a digging of heels) of the police force in this country. They have been promising they will do it.*
    B: ^c*(I'll have a word with them/Don't hold your breath/They have been outclassed/They are getting worked up about it)!*

11. A: *Your team were so* ^a*(panned out/glossed over/lapped up/sluggish) today. They looked like they had just got out of bed. We won two-nil, but it could really have been five.*
    B: *OK, OK. There's no need to* ^b*(outclass/gloat/muddle through/wince).*

138

Answers to Exercises

Chapter One

1(a) dressing-down; (b) step up; 2(a) heyday; (b) losing his marbles; 3(a) gift of the gab; (b) lose it; 4(a) plug; (b) lost the plot; 5(a) overlook; (b) blunders; 6(a) farce; (b) gulf; 7(a) doing yourself down; (b) turn your life around; 8(a) In the wake of; (b) backlash; 9(a) moping; (b) take the bull by the horns; 10(a) step down; (b) tight-lipped; 11(a) wary; (b) craves; 12(a) Banish; (b) mug's game; 13 (a) cutting edge; (b) opt out of; 14 (a) gruelling; (b) sparked; 15 (a) deterred; (b) knee-jerk.

Chapter Two

1(a) stifling; (b) overhauled; 2(a) brace; (b) spate; 3(a) renowned; (b) tantrums; (c) turn a blind eye 4(a) in mourning; (b) mellow; 5(a) bickering; (b) depleted; 6(a) vulnerable; (b) burden; 7(a) flattered; (b) feat; 8(a) striving; (b) stark; (c) in the limelight 9(a) hell broke loose; (b) seething; 10(a) fat cats; (b) underhand; 11(a) Deploying; (b) outlawed; 12(a) dismayed; (b) lure; 13(a) poised; (b) busybody; 14(a) gloom; (b) covered-up..

Chapter Three

1(a) step in; (b) hard-liners; 2(a) killing; (b) tatters; 3(a) its toll; (b) rallied round; (c) stunned; 4(a) vindictive; (b) my cup of tea; 5(a) implemented; (b) sets in; (c) wreak havoc; 6(a) Commiserations; (b) gathering momentum; (c) reimburse; 7(a) downfall; (b) going with the flow; (c) flogging a dead horse; 8(a) deplore; (b) last resort; 9(a) step down; (b) Rather you than me; 10(a) clinch; (b) heads will roll; 11(a) livelihood; (b) chip in; 12(a) stick to your guns; (b) fake.

Chapter Four

1(a) out of the woods; (b) the horse's mouth; 2(a) field day; (b) palaver; 3(a) underdog; (b) chip on his shoulder; 4(a) pull his weight; (b) fobbed me off; 5(a) easily led; (b) ring a bell; 6(a) steal his thunder; (b) bat an eyelid; (c) petty 7(a) godsend; (b) bode well; 8(a) lived up to; (b) uplifting; 9(a) bingeing; (b) work cut out; 10(a) roped into; (b) neck and neck; 11(a) on tenterhooks; (b) took the liberty of; (c) shrewd; 12(a) fads; (b) set in my ways; 13(a) reek; (b) plodded on; 14(a) bowled over; (b) bail out.

Chapter Five

1(a) rule of thumb; (b) ruffles my feathers; (c) rise to the bait; 2(a) excruciating; (b) an ordeal; (c) humour; 3(a) ring-fenced; (b) reading between the lines; (c) detractors; 4(a) knack; (b) corny;; (c) taking the biscuit 5(a) sit through; (b) pass the buck; (c) come to their senses; 6(a) rekindled; (b) spurred on; (c) role reversal; 7(a) boycott; (b) don't blame you;; (c) the penny has dropped; 8(a) uncanny; (b) close ranks: (c) sneer at; 9(a) much of a muchness; (b) do away with; (c) done and dusted; 10(a) red tape; (b) gloom; (c) peaking.

Chapter Six

1(a) feeling the pinch; (b) play it by ear; (c) vindicated; 2(a) recklessly; (b) squandering; (c) vilified; 3(a) in the nick of time; (b) disarray; (c) bleary-eyed; 4(a) an upheaval; (b) mount up; (c) The jury is still out; 5(a) bereft; (b) red herring; (c) beggars belief; 6 (a) soften the blow; (b) put on a brave face; (c) hastily; 7(a) clash; (b) shortcomings; (c) pulling me up; 8(a) stickler; (b) gall; (c) put him in his place; 9(a) unveiled; (b) insight; (c) an accident waiting to happen; 10(a) in the same boat; (b) fallen from grace; (c) got our just deserts.

Chapter Seven

1(a) groggy; (b) looming; (c) grumbling; 2(a) enshrined; (b) an overriding; (c) demise; 3(a) come with strings attached; (b) knock-on-effect; (c) flick through them; 4(a) level-headed; (b) buck the trend; (c) flavour of the month; 5(a) on the chin; (b) in a huff; (c) mull over; 6(a) littered with; (b) rein in; 7(a) no love lost; (b) way off the mark; (c) struck a chord; 8(a) ducking the issue; (b) The bottom line; (c) undercut; 9(a) whitewash; (b) Par for the course; (c) bear the brunt; 10(a) vicious circle; (b) tick all the right boxes; (c) get the ball rolling.

Chapter Eight

1(a) take a swipe at him; (b) Credit where credit's due; (c) overdo; 2(a) rant; (b) cutting off your nose to spite your face; (c) fester; 3(a) delving into; (b) shrinking violet; (c) take my hat off to; 4(a) take a tough stance against; (b) paid lip service to; (c) demonized; 5(a) short shrift; (b) ploughed back; (c) in awe of; 6(a) twiddling their thumbs; (b) take them to task; (c) sitting on; 7(a) alluding to; (b) overstretched; (c) flies in the face of; 8(a) sporadic; (b) milking it; (c) hunch; 9(a) unravel; (b) watershed; (c) tarnished; 10(a) alarm bells should have rung; (b) slashed; (c) nothing is set in stone.

Chapter Nine

1(a) rest on our laurels; (b) weather the storm; (c) few and far between; 2(a) outclassed; (b) half-hearted; (c) found wanting; 3(a) counting your blessings; (b) gone off the rails; (c) wince; 4(a) entrenched; (b) get together; (c) agree to disagree; 5(a) ticking over; (b) muddling through; (c) gloss over; 6(a) could have sworn; (b) get your act together; (c) smug; 7(a) digs her heels in; (b) worked up; (c) have a word with; 8(a) panders to; (b) lap it up; (c) muddled up; 9(a) fend for themselves; (b) blend in her; (c) pan out; 10(a) the tip of the iceberg; (b) root and branch reform; (c) Don't hold your breath; 11(a) sluggish; (b) gloat;

.

Index

LETTER **A**

ACCIDENT, 79
ACT (To get one's act together), 130
AGREE (To agree to disagree), 123
ALARM (To ring/sound alarm bells), 108
ALLUDE/ALLUSION, 116
APPETITE (To work up an appetite), 132
ATTACHED (To come with strings attached), 95
AWE (To be in awe of), 112

LETTER **B**

BACK LASH, 2
BAILOUT (To bail out/bailout), 51
BAIT (To rise to the bait), 59
BANISH, 11
BAT (Not bat/Without batting an eyelid), 52
BEAR (To bear the brunt of), 97
BEGGAR (To beggar belief), 83
BELIEF (To beggar belief), 83
BELL (To ring a bell), 49
          (To ring/sound alarm bells), 108
BEREFT, 83
BICKER, 15
BINGE 49
BISCUIT (To take the biscuit), 60
BLAME ("I don't blame you"), 59
BLEARY (Bleary-eyed), 86
BLESSING (To count one's blessings), 134
BLEND (To blend in), 122
BLIND (To turn a blind eye to), 16
BLOW (A blow), 77
BLUNDER, 5
BOAT (To be in the same boat), 80
BODE (To bode well), 52
BOTTOM (The bottom line, 101
BOWL (To bowl over), 43
BOYCOTT 60

BOXES (Box-ticking), 99
          (To tick all the right boxes), 99
BRACE (To brace oneself), 19
BRAVE (To put on a brave face), 80
BREAK (All hell broke loose), 16
BREATH (Not to hold your breath), 97
BRUNT (To bear the brunt of), 93
BUCK (To buck the trend), 68
          ("The buck stops with me"), 68
          (To pass the buck), 68
BULL (To take the bull by the horns), 5
BURDEN, 16
BUSYBODY, 19

LETTER **C**

CAT (Fat cat), 22
CHIN (To take it on the chin), 92
CHIP (To chip in), 38
          (To have a chip on one's shoulder), 46
CHORD (To strike a chord), 98
CIRCLE (Vicious circle), 100
CLASH, 75
CLICK, 131
CLINCH, 36
CLOSE (To close ranks), 64
COME (To come to one's senses), 65
          (To come with strings attached), 95
COMMISERATIONS, 36
CORNY, 63
COUNT (To count one's blessings), 134
COURSE (Par for the course), 95
COVER (Cover-up), 23
CRAVE/CRAVING, 7
CREDIT (Credit where credit's due, 107
CUP ("It's not my cup of tea"), 36
CUT (To cut off one's nose to spite one's face), 109
          (To have one's work cut out), 52
CUTTING-EDGE (To be at the cutting-edge of something), 11

LETTER **D**

DAY (To have a field day), 50
DELVE (To delve into), 107

DEMISE, 93
DEMONIZE, 108
DEPLETE/DEPLETED, 20
DEPLORE/DEPLORABLE, 32
DEPLOY, 19
DESERTS (To get one's just deserts), 84
DETER, 1
DETRACTOR, 66
DIG (To dig one's heels in), 125
DISAGREE (To agree to disagree), 123
DISARRAY, 76
DISMAYED, 19
DO (To do away with), 68
    (To do oneself down), 9
DONE (Done and dusted), 61
DOWNFALL, 33
DRAG (To drag one's heels), 125
DRESSING (To give someone a dressing down), 10
DROP (The penny has dropped), 65
DUCK (To duck the issue/question), 92
DUSTED (Done and dusted), 61

LETTER E
EAR (To play it by ear), 81
EASILY (Easily-led), 51
EFFECT (Knock-on-effect), 92
ENSHRINED, 98
ENTHUSIASM (To work up enthusiasm), 132
ENTRENCHED, 122
EXCRUCIATING, 63
EYE (To turn a blind eye to/towards), 16
EYED (Bleary-eyed), 86
EYELID (Not/Without batting an eyelid), 52

LETTER F
FACE (To cut off one's nose to spite one's face), 109
    (To fly in the face of), 116
    (To put on a brave face), 80
FAD, 43
FAKE, 29
FALL (To fall from/out of grace), 85
FAR (Few and far between), 128

FARCE/FARCICAL, 8
FAT (Fat cat), 22
FEAT, 24
FEATHER (To ruffle one's feathers), 67
FEEL (To feel the pinch), 77
FENCE (To ring-fence), 59
FEND (To fend for), 128
FESTER, 109
FEW (Few and far between), 128
FIELD (To have a field day), 50
FIND (To find wanting), 127
FLATTER/FLATTERY, 18
FLAVOUR (Flavour of the month), 94
FLICK (To flick through), 96
FLIP (To flip through), 96
FLOG (To flog a dead horse), 34
FLOW (To go with the flow), 33
FLY (To fly in the face of), 116
FOB (To fob off), 49

LETTER G
GALL/GALLING, 83
GATHER (To gather pace/momentum), 32
GEL, 131
GET (To get on one's high horse), 47
    (To get one's act together), 130
    (To get one's just deserts), 84
    (To get short shrift from), 110
    (To get the ball rolling), 99
    (To get worked up about/over something), 132
GIFT (To have the gift of the gab), 7
GIVE (To give free rein to), 101
    (To give someone a dressing down), 10
GLOAT, 123
GLOOM/GLOOMY, 63
GLOSS (To gloss over), 125
GLUM, 23
GO (To go off the rails), 125
    (To go with the flow), 33
GODSEND, 43
GRACE (To fall out of grace), 85
GROGGY, 96
GRUELLING, 3
GRUMBLE, 91

GULF, 3
GUNS (To stick to one's guns), 36

LETTER H
HALF (Half-hearted), 123
HAPPEN (An accident waiting to happen), 79
HARD-LINE/HARD-LINER, 30
HASTY, 83
HAT (To take one's hat off to), 108
HAVE (To have a chip on one's shoulder), 46
    (To have a field day), 50
    (To have the gift of the gab), 7
    (To have a knack for), 65
    (To have one's work cut out), 52
    (To have a word with someone), 129
HAVOC (To wreak havoc), 37
HEADS (Heads will roll), 38
HEADED (Level-headed), 91
HEELS (To dig one's heels in), 125
HELL (All hell broke loose), 16
HERRING (Red herring), 75
HEYDAY, 1
HIGH (To get on one's high horse), 47
HOLD (Not to hold your breath), 124
HORNS (To take the bull by the horns), 5
HORSE (To flog a dead horse), 34
    (To get on one's high horse), 47
HUFF (In a huff), 99
HUMOUR (To humour someone), 65
HUNCH, 114

LETTER I
ICEBERG (Tip of the iceberg), 133
IMPLEMENT, 32
INSIGHT/INSIGHTFUL, 78
ISSUE (To duck the issue), 92

LETTER J
JURY (The jury is still out), 78
JUST (To get one's just deserts), 84

LETTER K
KEEP (To keep tight-lipped about something), 1

KILLING (To make a killing), 31
KNACK (To have a knack for), 65
KNEE (Knee jerk), 1
KNOCK (Knock-on-effect), 92

LETTER L
LAP (To lap up), 128
LAURELS (To rest on one's laurels), 122
LED (Easily led), 51
LEVEL (Level-headed), 91
LIBERTIES (To take liberties), 44
    (To take the liberty of), 44
LIMELIGHT, 15
LINE (The bottom line), 101
LINES (To read between the lines), 67
LIP (To pay lip service), 115
LIPPED (To keep tight-lipped about something), 1
LITTERED, 92
LIVE (to live up to), 49
LIVELIHOOD, 32
LOOM, 98
LOSE (To lose it), 4
    (To lose one's marbles), 10
    (To lose the plot), 10
LOVE ("There's no love lost between them"), 95
LURE, 22

LETTER M
MAKE (To make a killing), 31
MARBLES (To lose one's marbles), 10
MARK (To be way off the mark), 96
MELLOW, 17
MILK (To milk it), 111
MOMENTUM (To gather momentum), 32
MONTH (Flavour of the month), 94
MOPE, 9
MOUNT (To mount up), 82
MOURN/MOURNING, 20
MUCH (much of a muchness), 62
MUDDLE (To muddle through), 126
    (To muddle up), 126
MUG, 3

MULL (To mull over), 94

LETTER **N**
NECK (To be neck and neck), 54
NICK (In the nick of time), 81

LETTER **O**
OPT, 10
ORDEAL, 62
OUT (To be out of the woods), 52
OUTCLASS, 129
OUTLAW/OUTLAWED, 22
OVERDO, 107
OVERHAUL, 23
OVERLOOK, 5
OVERRIDE, 91
OVERSTRETCHED, 111

LETTER **P**
PACE (To gather pace), 32
PALAVER, 45
PAN (To pan out), 134
PANDER (To pander to), 133
PAR (par for the course), 95
PASS (To pass the buck), 68
PAY (To pay lip service to), 115
PEAK (To peak), 70
PENNY (The penny has dropped), 65
PETTY, 47
PINCH (To feel the pinch), 77
PLAY (To play it by ear), 81
PLACE (To put someone in their place), 84
PLOD (To plod on/through), 45
PLOT (To lose the plot), 10
PLOUGH (To plough back), 116
PLUG (To plug), 6
POISED (To be poised to do something), 23
PULL (To pull one's weight), 51
    (To pull someone up on something), 77
PUT (To put on a brave face), 80
    (To put someone in their place), 84

LETTER **Q**
QUESTION (To duck the question),92

LETTER **R**
RAILS (To go off the rails), 125
RALLY (To rally round), 30
RANKS (To close ranks), 64
RANT, 114
RASH, 83
RATHER ("Rather you than me"), 35
READ (To read between the lines), 67
RECKLESS, 84
RED (Red herring), 75
    (Red tape), 67
REEK (To reek of), 47
REFORM (Root and branch reform), 131
REIMBURSE, 29
REIN (To rein in), 101
    (To give free rein to), 101
REKINDLE, 67
RENOWNED (To be renowned for), 25
RESORT (To resort to), 35
REST (To rest on one's laurels), 122
REVENGE (To wreak revenge), 37
REVERSAL (Role reversal), 60
RING (To ring alarm bells), 108
    (To ring a bell), 49
    (To ring-fence), 59
RISE (To rise to the bait), 59
ROLE (Role reversal), 60
ROLL (Heads will roll), 38
ROLLING (To get the ball rolling), 99
ROOT (Root and branch reform), 130
ROPE (To rope someone in), 45
RUFFLE (To ruffle one's feathers), 67
RULE (Rule of thumb), 69

LETTER **S**
SEETHING, 15
SENSES (To come to one's senses), 65
SERVICE (To pay lip service to), 115
SET (To be set in one's ways), 43
    (To set the ball rolling), 99
    (To set in), 30
    (To set in stone), 113
SHORT (To get short shrift from), 110

SHORTCOMINGS, 81
SHOULDER (To have a chip on one's shoulder), 46
SHREWD, 50
SHRIFT (To get short shrift from), 110
SHRINKING (Shrinking violet), 115
SIT (To sit on something), 111
    (To sit through), 63
SLASH, 110
SLUGGISH, 130
SMUG, 127
SNEER (To sneer at), 63
SOUND (To sound alarm bells), 108
SPARK (To spark), 4
SPATE, 23
SPITE (To cut off one's nose to spite one's face), 109
SPORADIC, 108
SPUR (To spur on), 69
SQUANDER, 82
SQUIRM, 127
STANCE, 113
STARK, 15
STEAL (To steal someone's thunder), 48
STEP (To step down), 7
        (To step in), 30
        (To step something up), 7
        (To step up to the plate/challenge), 7
STICK (To stick to one's guns), 36
STICKLER, 75
STIFLE/STIFLING, 18
STORM (To weather the storm), 129
STRIKE (To strike a chord), 98
STRINGS (To come with strings attached), 95
STRIVE, 18
STUNNED/STUNNING, 29
SWIPE (To take a swipe at), (107
SWORN ("I could have sworn"), 132

LETTER T

TAKE (To take the biscuit), 60
        (To take the bull by the horns), 5
        (To take it on the chin), 92
        (To take its toll on), 29
        (To take the liberties), 44
(To take the liberty of), 44
(To take one's hat off to), 108
(To take someone to task), 114
(To take a swipe at),107
(To take a tough stance against), 113
TANTRUM, 17
TAPE (Red tape), 67
TARNISH, 110
TATTERS (In tatters), 35
TEA ("It's not my cup of tea"), 36
TENTERHOOKS, 45
THUMB (Rule of thumb), 69
THUMBS (To twiddle one's thumbs), 110
THUNDER (To steal someone's thunder), 48
TICK (To tick all the right boxes), 99
        (To tick over), 132
TIGHT-LIPPED (To keep tight-lipped), 1
TIME (In the nick of time), 81
TIP (Tip of the iceberg), 133
TREND (To buck the trend), 93
TURN (To turn a blind eye to), 16
        (To turn something round), 9
TWIDDLE (To twiddle one's thumbs), 110

LETTER U

UNCANNY, 68
UNDERCUT, 94
UNDERDOG, 54
UNDERHAND, 16
UNRAVEL, 117
UNVEILED, 80
UPHEAVAL, 80
UPLIFTING, 53

LETTER V

VICIOUS (Vicious circle), 100
VILIFY, 84
VINDICATED, 77
VINDICTIVE, 33
VIOLET (Shrinking violet), 115
VULNERABLE, 20

LETTER W

WAKE (In the wake of), 8

WANTING (To find wanting), 127
WARY (To be wary of), 5
WATERSHED, 114
WAY (To be way off the mark), 96
WAYS (To set in one's ways), 43
WEATHER (To weather the storm), 129
WEIGHT (To pull one's weight), 51
WHITEWASH, 99
WINCE, 127
WOODS (To be out of the woods), 52
WORD (To have a word with someone), 129
WORK (To get worked up about/over), 132
        (To have one's work cut out), 52
        (To work up an appetite), 132
        (To work up enthusiasm), 132
WREAK (To wreak havoc), 37
        (To wreak revenge), 37

CD Index Card	
Track	Page
1. Author's Introduction (not in book)	
2. A newspaper article about public transport in London	12
3. News bulletin	26
4. Conversation between two doctors-General Practitioners (GPs)	39
5. A passage from an autobiography	55
6. Two mothers having a chat outside their children's school	71
7. TV morning news programme with journalists reviewing the newspapers	87
8. Exchange of informal emails between client and web designer	102
9. Prime Minister's speech to students	118
10. Headmistress's speech at school open day	135